gardendecorator

garden decorator
making the most of outdoor space

gilly love

LAUREL
GLEN

For Stephen Harrington, an extraordinary friend

First published in North America in 2000 by

Laurel Glen Publishing

An imprint of the Advantage Publishers Group

5880 Oberlin Drive, San Diego, CA 92121

www.advantagebooksonline.com

Text copyright © Gilly Love 2000

Design and layout copyright © Conran Octopus

Project photographs © Linda Burgess 2000

Project designs © Gilly Love 2000

Produced by Conran Octopus Ltd., 2–4 Heron Quays,
London E14 4JP

Commissioning editor: Stuart Cooper

Assistant editor: Lucy Nicholson

Senior editor: Emma Clegg

Copy editor: Judy Cox

Proofreader: Colette Campbell

Designer: Sue Storey

Picture research: Liz Boyd

Production controller: Sue Bayliss

ISBN 1-57145-667-8

Library of Congress Cataloging in Publication Data available
upon request.

Color origination by Sang Choy International, Singapore

Printed in China.

1 2 3 4 5   00 01 02 03 04

CONTENTS

INTRODUCTION

Today's gardens are for people who really want to enjoy their outside space. *Garden Decorator* is therefore not a traditional gardening manual—it is a book about designing gardens as extensions to the home, with the emphasis on outdoor living rather than horticulture. You do not even need a garden to provide that vital link with the outdoors. A tiny balcony, a rooftop terrace, or a concrete basement all have fantastic potential for providing extra space and spiritual comfort. What really matters is that you create a space where you feel comfortable and where the design works for you and your family, just like every other room in your home.

The contemporary garden can be a place to relax in peace and enjoy the sensory delights that only the natural world can provide, whether this means an area for alfresco dining with family and friends or a secluded seat surrounded by aromatic plants. In any outdoor living space, comfort and practicality should be the primary considerations—and simple designs and natural materials will always work best. Focal points such as a beautiful tree can illustrate the changing seasons; or a bed filled with huge sunflowers can recall happy childhood memories; and even the smallest water feature can provide either an exhilarating cascade or a soft, sensuous gurgle. Judicious lighting will create magic, drama and romance, and evenings spent outside can be as fulfilling as days.

If you choose flowers and plants that truly echo your personality you can make this space yours forever. Use them to enhance the room's design and you will create a style and atmosphere that will change from one season to another— your garden is one room that will never lose its capacity to charm and surprise. Select plants that complement your lifestyle and have the confidence to experiment from season to season. Enthusiastic cooks will delight in growing fresh herbs or even homegrown fruit and vegetables; others will want flowers and foliage to bring indoors. Some people will need a minimalist atmosphere to enjoy stress-free relaxation, while others will find that they prefer a time-consuming space where they can lose themselves for hours, utterly absorbed in growing, tending, and watering.

Whatever you choose to do, your outside room will be unique—a special place to refresh your spirits, calm your nerves, and feed your soul. *Garden Decorator* will help you create personal space where you can truly be yourself.

assessing your garden

Designing your own garden is a challenging adventure, an opportunity to discover and appreciate the world around you. The most successful interiors have one element in common—they are designed specifically for the people who live in them. The same good design principles of form and function, planning, and detail are essential ingredients for creating gardens that are truly personalized spaces.

LEFT   A contemporary interpretation of the potager, or kitchen garden, which was the 1999 theme of the Festival International des Jardins at Chaumont-sur-Loire, France.

Your connection to the outdoor world may be achieved by means of a garden, a roof terrace, a balcony, or even a window box, but on whatever level it is pitched, this provides a vital link to nature. At a time when the world has few truly wild places remaining, we are becoming very concerned about nature, conservation, and ecology, and this has made us appreciate our gardens more than ever before.

Modern gardeners are often not experienced horticulturalists but people who appreciate the sensory satisfaction of enjoying their own outside space. We all need a special place of peace and tranquillity, a private little piece of paradise. If we have no access to the outside world and cannot relish the sights, sounds, and smells of the changing seasons, we deny ourselves contact with nature and a real understanding of the need to protect and value our fragile environment. Nearly a decade ago the English garden designer John Brookes wrote: "The garden is still, as it ever was, a retreat, but it is no longer a retreat from the 'awefulness' of Nature; rather it is a retreat from the awfulness of the twentieth-century manifestations of Man himself."

Over the centuries garden design has been subject to great changes of style, and shifts in the way that nature has been perceived and interpreted. Many contemporary gardens are inspired by the concept of the paradise garden, a legacy of the Islamic style, in which the garden was an enclosed sanctuary filled with the sight and sound of water and shade, a place set apart from the harshness of the desert beyond its walls. Replace the scorching desert with the urban jungle of busy streets and traffic jams, and it is easy to see that we, too, need an oasis of peace and quiet.

Other historical influences are the gardens of medieval monasteries, which were built around a cloistered quadrangle, imitating the architecture of Roman villas. These enclosed gardens produced medicinal herbs for the infirmaries, and flowers for garlands and festivals. They are the ancestors of modern herb gardens, where we can also grow fresh organic vegetables in pots and containers.

Contemporary gardens, above all, are an extension of the home, with house and garden intrinsically linked. The garden may be a small terrace or balcony, or a series of interconnected spaces that can be perceived as outside "rooms."

The key to its success has as much to do with careful planning and design awareness as with horticultural training.

Trees, plants, and shrubs are nevertheless an important design element and are vital in creating a mood or emphasizing a particular style. To get ideas, you can visit gardens, read books, and seek advice from reputable nurseries.

Left: A sunbaked wall and stone banquette surrounded by aromatic planting provide a place of quiet seclusion. A couple of sheets that are suspended on thin poles look more appropriate in this relaxed setting than a more formal parasol.

Above: Perhaps the most important element of this Mediterranean garden is its breathtaking view. A low wall defines the terrace perimeter, with dense evergreen planting on either side, producing an effective windbreak.

A room with a view

Space, proportion, and natural light are the most important ingredients of modern living, quite independent of fashion or style. The decision we make when choosing a house or apartment to live in involves practical considerations such as location, cost, and size, but the perfect home also needs to engender the right feeling for us.

You can make structural changes to increase the size and improve the function of individual rooms, but it is not possible to change the outlook from windows and, more importantly, the light they receive. Homes without windows would be impossible to live in—we all need natural light for our bodies to function healthily, and sunlight creates a feeling of optimism that lifts our spirits. Rooms with a view command a premium in hotels because your enjoyment of a vacation is dramatically affected if you wake up every morning greeted by a stunning view, as opposed to the sight of a brick wall outside the window. Few of us are lucky enough to have a home surrounded by beautiful countryside, but the outlook is always an important consideration.

When buying a house, look out at the views from the windows and observe the type of light they receive. You will probably not have the opportunity to view it in every season, but it is sound advice to walk around the property at different times of day and night. Note where the light comes in and for how long it remains inside and, just as important, outside. Most homes do not face one direction exactly, and the quality and quantity of natural light can often be affected by other buildings, walls, or trees. The quantity of light may be easily improved if it is impeded by a vigorous climber or overhanging branches that obscure a window, but you can hardly demolish your next-door-neighbor's house or the five-story school opposite.

Right: The clean lines of the modern architecture, the wide expanses of glass, and a crisp mesh metal panel are all reflected in the still, shallow pool, which improves the humidity in this enclosed space.

Below: This perfect solution for a basement dining room, which seamlessly merges into the garden is achieved by using the same colors and materials for both the interior and exterior floors and walls.

Right: Effective shelter and shade are vital when creating an outside room, and this veranda basks in the warmth of the sun, while also being shaded from the discomfort of overhead glare. An exterior water source is another essential feature, along with an outside light that clearly illuminates the entrance.

Extending space

If your potential new home is in need of improvement and if finances and local building codes permit, a roof terrace, garden room extension, or patio will provide an outside living space. Even replacing a window can make an enormous difference, particularly if it is one that gives access to the outdoors. In older houses the kitchen and basement have often become the central living area, a combined kitchen and dining space that seamlessly spills out into the garden. A dining room that overlooks a garden will be completely transformed by the addition of fully glazed French doors. The light in the room is dramatically improved, whatever the season, and when the weather is warm and the doors are opened the garden or terrace becomes an integral part of the home, rather than a separate space. It is a functional juxtaposition of inside and outside space specifically designed for people to live in comfortably all year round.

Choosing a style

The style you choose for your outside space is an entirely personal one; whether you go for fashionable colors, understated simplicity, or classical style depends on your individual taste. You could project a fantasy image of how you see yourself, or alternatively a true and honest picture of your character and lifestyle. Fashion and social change have dictated the style of how rooms have been designed and decorated and then rearranged and altered. It is too early to find a label for the first century of the third millennium, but there is a powerful desire to put aside convention and to shape inside and outside "rooms" to meet the needs of their owners. Forget the notion that a garden is just a place for plants—plants are an essential element, but not the sole reason for a garden to exist. Consider more carefully the need for an outside room to cook and eat in, a place to work and read, a private area to play and relax in.

Below: A tubular steel pergola is the framework for a temporary canvas canopy, which can easily be adjusted according to the sun's position. Low Japanese-style benches follow the shape of the terrace, not impeding the surrounding view.

Glass rooms—the options

One of the most attractive ways of combining living indoors with outside pleasures is to extend your home with a sunroom, or conservatory. Historically, conservatory structures became viable only in the eighteenth century, when developments in the manufacture of glass permitted the construction of hothouses and orangeries. These rooms were inspired by a romantic notion of worshiping nature, which began in France and spread very rapidly among the privileged classes of Europe. Conservatories were designed to show off tender plants and flowers to dramatic effect, and to impress and entertain. They exuded pleasure, leisure, and conspicuous wealth, and were rooms in which homeowners could feel in contact with nature while being protected from the weather. These glass spaces had very little in common with the more functional demands of other rooms in the house.

Traditional conservatories were designed for plants and provided a high level of humidity which was not comfortable for people. However, the concept of the glasshouse has survived several hundred years, to be revived and reinvented to provide a practical living space that integrates harmoniously with existing architecture rather than a superfluous room tacked on to the side of a building. Thanks to modern building techniques and the sophistication of glass technology, it is possible to construct a glass room on any level, facing any aspect, and for it to provide a comfortable living environment all year round. To achieve this, meticulous planning and good construction are essential, including double-glazing, toughened safety glass, effective ventilation, and security locks on doors and opening windows.

Right: Removing part of a kitchen wall opens up and incorporates space from what would otherwise be a redundant outside corridor. This makes space for a dining area with a glazed ceiling and an open view of the garden beyond.

The shape of the interior of a conservatory can have a dramatic effect on the space available. Bay-shaped designs will limit where you can place furniture, for example, and although an octagonal room may look attractive, it will inevitably prove much more difficult to furnish than a simple, regular shape. The direction in which a conservatory faces creates very different demands on the way the room is heated and cooled. North-facing glass rooms require very efficient heating in winter, whereas a south-facing conservatory may be oppressively hot in summer unless its roof is shaded and it is equipped with fully opening doors and windows. These extremes of temperature, that are rarely encountered in other rooms, will make a conservatory either a practical living space or a "no-go" area for much of the year.

So is a conservatory the right solution? A fully glazed room with sensitive temperature control and high humidity is a paradise for many plants. Conservatories can make even the slowest-growing tropical plants develop to their full potential, but they may, in this confined space, be more susceptible to insect infestation and require regular spraying with pesticides. For the dedicated plant collector and gardener, a conservatory is ideal; it is the perfect environment in which to raise seeds, to overwinter tender specimens, and to grow exotic plants that flower all year round.

You can still be true to nature and enjoy the comforts of modern living by creating a partially glazed extension where the plants inside are just accessories, the garden outside feels more intimate, and there is a natural flow from house to garden.

Above: The style and character of the interior furnishings and colors are echoed in the tones and textures of the paving, planting, and garden trellis.

Left: From the garden looking back at the conservatory, harmony prevails. Because the glazing is restricted to the front elevation and central roof lantern light, the extension to this English house remains cool in summer.

Research and planning

Consulting a reputable architect is a wise decision when contemplating major structural changes, and he or she will be able to explain the possibilities and also any restrictions. Construction may involve removing some, if not all, of the rear elevation of a building, but widening a doorway or eliminating part of a wall could drastically improve the natural light and space in existing rooms, as well as improving the air flow and ventilation in the extension.

Many successful contemporary garden rooms have glazed roofs with solid walls, and if the ceiling height is raised to construct a lantern roof, this creates a well-proportioned space, filled with natural light and moving shadows that subtly change from season to season. When such rooms are well designed, often combined with a kitchen, they provide an attractive space for living, cooking, and eating. A practical kitchen benefits from having a casual dining space that is linked to both the cooking and preparation area and to the garden. Provided it is built to the highest standards of insulation and ventilation, condensation is not a problem and most modern kitchen furniture will not fade even when subjected to direct sunlight.

Modern sunrooms need to function like any other room in the home, so their decorative scheme calls for an approach that blends the garden with the house. The plain, bright white favored by the Victorians for their conservatories is not the most sympathetic color to choose today. A combination of warm and neutral tones is easier to live with, and these colors will blend more harmoniously with your exterior masonry.

Terra cotta floor tiles used to be a popular traditional choice for flooring, but unless they are well weathered and faded, a large expanse of orange can be difficult to live with and will restrict other decorating decisions. A good way to make a modern extension blend with older architecture is to lay a reclaimed floor, which makes up for the lack of architectural features and provides instant character. The softer, more subtle, neutral hues of limestone, creamy marble, or bleached bricks echo the contemporary taste for natural-toned carpets and sisal matting.

A wooden floor, either naturally colored or stained, will blend perfectly with exterior decking in natural honey-colored treated pine or a darker and more expensive Western red cedar hardwood. Decking is a practical choice, particularly if you need to raise the outside ground level to match that of the interior, and it is a warm and friendly surface for children and for bare feet.

Flooring in a sunroom does not need to exactly match its adjoining exterior, but it makes for a more seamless transition if it is of a similar tone. It also makes practical sense to have an area of hard surface between this room and the garden.

Below: An enclosed outside space can reflect the atmosphere of its surroundings by using sympathetic colors.

Consulting a garden designer

Once you step outside, your design and decorating confidence may begin to falter. Before you make any major decisions, a consultation with a professional garden designer could prevent both heartache and costly mistakes. An experienced and sensitive designer will try to interpret your ideas and requirements, and also to present you with ways and means of how to achieve them successfully.

Allay the fear that a professional will take over the project and present you with a colossal invoice. You may decide that all you need is a plan that you can execute yourself within your own timescale. One advantage of employing a competent designer is that he or she will have firsthand experience of good contractors for both hard and soft land-

Left: This rooftop garden in Manhattan was undoubtedly designed to be seen rather than walked upon. The Japanese-inspired landscape of bronze galvanized strips are decoratively infilled with a mat-forming sedum and smooth river stones.

scaping, plus knowledge of reputable nurseries. Many garden centers employ their own designers, and although they tend to specify their own plants and products, they are an economical way of starting from scratch. Some gardening magazines offer a postal design service, and for a reasonable fee you can get lots of ideas for your garden without any further obligation.

It can be extremely comforting and reassuring to commission a garden designer at least for an initial site visit. Besides being able to see their portfolio of previous projects—a good indicator of both their skill and imagination—you will receive an evaluation of your space and its aspect, soil, location, and climatic implications. Make the most of this visit by preparing a list of questions you want to ask and walk around with them. Help the designer, too, by compiling a selection of pictures that you are inspired by. They could be your own photographs of gardens and landscapes you have seen or pictures taken from books and magazines, but they will give the designer a clear indication of your preferred style and aspirations.

The most successful design schemes, both inside and out, often evolve from a single idea or inspiration. Garden designers generally have a very

Far left: A half-curtain of sky-blue glass beads frames the entrance to this plant-filled London roof terrace. In summer the datura and lavender fill this tiny space with sweet fragrance.

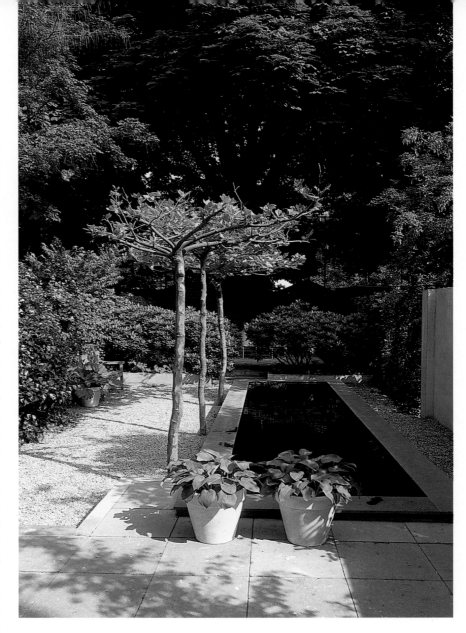

definite style of their own, and this is why people are drawn to them in the first place, but when it comes to advising clients, a good designer should concentrate on the needs and personalities of the client rather than trying to impose their own personal taste.

If you do decide to employ a designer to produce a detailed design, you need to have first-hand experience of their approach if you are to build a successful relationship. More input from you will make for a more appropriate scheme. Take note of the questions they ask you as an indication of their professionalism. They should inquire about the lifestyles of the people who will use the outside space. Busy people with demanding jobs may prefer a low-maintenance garden that can be enjoyed especially in the evenings, which may be their only opportunity to appreciate it apart from weekends. Outdoor decking would create a low-maintenance platform for dining and entertaining, and evening-scented plants and an attractive lighting scheme would make the most of summer twilight. With a powerful patio heater, which resembles a giant hurricane lamp, you could eat alfresco even in cool seasons.

Small children, or plans to have a family in the near future, will have a significant influence on a design. Avoid ponds or water features that children could topple into, and make sure that flooring is soft and warm underfoot and that any planting is robust and free of thorns or spiky leaves. If you are away from home regularly, you may want to consider fail-safe security arrangements, a timer-controlled irrigation system, or drought-friendly trees and shrubs. If you are always away in July, for example, avoid flowers and plants, bush fruits, and vegetables that reach their peak then and are at their most demanding. A garden should be designed to suit you without you having to be a slave to your sweet peas and lettuces.

Garden designers will inevitably ask you about your budget. Be prepared and be honest. If you are to create a fully functional outdoor room, you should

compare it to designing and building a kitchen from scratch, so you need to allocate the level of budget you would set aside for that. The implementation of most garden plans can be spread over a period of months, even years. Most interior designers will agree that, however tight the budget, they will apportion a significant amount of it to the flooring, and the same applies to an outside room. In small spaces, an outside room may need only one flooring material if it is to be in proportion with the rooms of the house.

Space planning is vital when you are preparing the blueprint for a terrace, and it has to be big enough to meet the demands you plan for it. As it is adjacent to the house, it is usually the obvious

Above: This slightly elevated view shows how a simple but well-proportioned design is transformed into a pleasing pattern of hard landscaping and structural planting.

Right: Mature trees are integrated into this bold and extroverted garden design. In this way the eye is encouraged to look farther than the perimeter wall to the landscape beyond.

place for entertaining, so you have to consider seating, space for a dining table, and room to move around it. Electricity and water are other design elements that need consideration before laying a solid floor. Even if your current budget does not allow for artificial lighting, a water feature, or an irrigation system, the conduits for power and water can be laid to be connected at a later date. It would be foolish to design an outside room without an exterior faucet, for example, and it needs to be thoroughly insulated unless the climate is warm all year round. The pipework can run up the side of the building or be attached to a boundary wall.

Whether you are engaging a designer or undertaking the project yourself, it costs nothing to take your time when making decisions. Whatever you choose to do will become part of your life for the foreseeable future. We can all afford to make the mistake of trying to grow a plant in the wrong place or in the wrong soil; this kind of error can easily be rectified and, if not, a plant's demise can be put down to the learning process of gardening. Erecting a cheap trellis that falls down in the first strong wind or employing a contractor who lays a paved terrace with no fall, so that it doesn't drain properly after rain, are expensive and irritating experiences,

time consuming and costly to remedy. Good design is just as important as horticultural supremacy, so on the first warm and sunny day of the year, when you feel an uncontrollable desire to spend a fortune at the nearest garden center, stop and think for a minute. Plants and flowers are the finishing touches to an outside room, an essential element, but only within the framework of a well-conceived design. They are, however, often the instant gratification you need when work is in progress. A window box brimming with scented hyacinths may raise your spirits when the garden is being excavated and your view is one of cement mixers and piles of bricks.

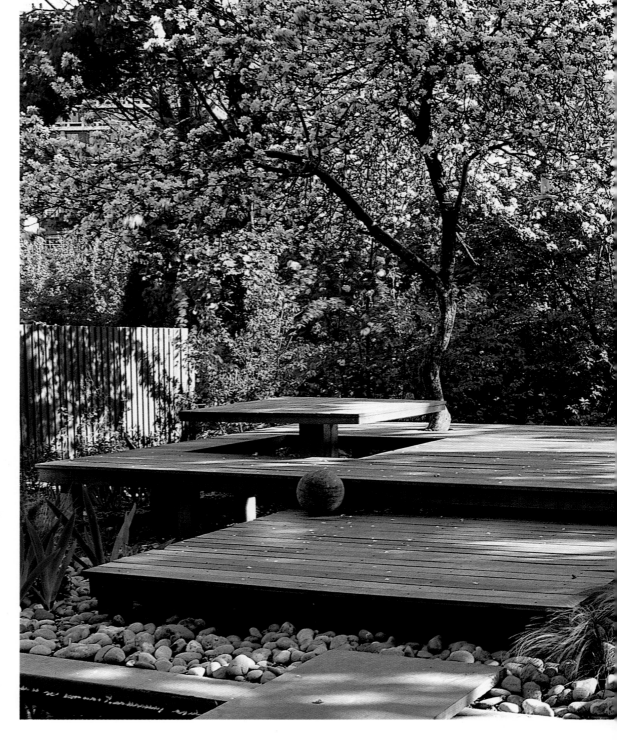

Lumber decking that is constructed on a series of interconnected levels solves the problem of sloping land, making a smooth visual transition between the house and its woodland surroundings. The mellow tone of the natural wooden floor is perfectly complemented by the channels of weed-suppressing pebbles and fine shingle from which silky tufts of grasses sprout up like green fountains.

Styles and inspirations

Identifying what you have in terms of site, climate, and aspect and deciding what you want to enjoy within this outside space are the building blocks for creating an original and personal Eden. Style is completely individual, but there are bound to be like-minded people whose ideas and designs you will be inspired by.

Modernist outdoor rooms are an update on minimalist interiors, so if you prefer uncluttered spaces with pared-down detail that engender a sense of calmness and tranquillity, you may be attracted to the austere influence of Le Corbusier. This controversial architect of the 1920s was a keen advocate of roof terraces, and incorporated them as an integral part of many of his municipal housing and private domestic commissions. Experiment with modern, streamlined floors; boundaries created by concrete and decking interspersed with pebbles and fine shingle; extensive use of still water in curved or geometric pools; structural plants in galvanized or shiny metal containers; and low-voltage lighting sunk into the ground or around the edges of water features.

A more eclectic approach would be to adapt influences and ideas gleaned from all over the world. Global travel has given us the opportunity to experience a diverse wealth of art and crafts, architecture, and landscapes. Drought-friendly Mediterranean planting on terraced gravel, intimate groves of rustling Japanese bamboo, wind chimes, and trickling water suit the ancient philosophy of feng shui, while huge terra cotta pots, or *pithoi,* from Crete, and giant Burmese water urns can be used to make dramatic garden sculptures. A collection of these elements creates a melting pot of familiar and foreign, antique and new. A piece of sculpture, the beauty of an existing tree, or an irrepressible desire to build an authentic Caribbean *casita,* may be the focus for an original design. Turning your garden into a haven for bees and birds, or an organic allotment for fruit and vegetables, is also within the realms of possibility.

If you find yourself short of ideas, get out and visit inspirational gardens, parks, exhibitions, festivals or anyplace where outside space is used creatively. Contemporary craftspeople, painters, and sculptors are producing installations, furniture, and ornamental features that represent refreshing new views of garden making. There is a wealth of inspiration once you start looking. If it is the cutting edge of innovative garden design you crave, then the place to go is the Festival International des Jardins at the Château de Chaumont-sur-Loire in France, held every year between June and October. Since 1992, part of the park of Chaumont has been dedicated to the garden of the twenty-first century. Jacques Wirtz, the acclaimed Belgian designer, has devised a pattern of 30 individual spaces, each approximately 275 yd. (250 m) square and enclosed by beech hedges, and landscape designers and artists from all over the world are invited to create a garden on a particular theme, which changes each year. Some of the gardens have been so successful and popular that they have been kept and are meticulously maintained.

One garden that has inspired me more than any other is the extraordinary space created by the late Derek Jarman, painter, theater designer, film maker, and passionate gardener from childhood. His garden surrounds a wooden fisherman's cottage on the shingle at Dungeness in Kent, England, a bleak place on a triangular stretch of land bordered by the sea on two sides. The surrounding landscape is gorse and pebbles, with the nuclear power plant looming in the distance.

In the inhospitable climate of salty winds and pervading sea mists, and from 1986 until his death in 1994, Jarman produced a personal landscape without visible boundaries, combining the indigenous plants of the area with traditional seashore plants such as angelica, lavender, rosemary, santolina, and erysimum. Stones and pebbles gathered from the shoreline, sorted by color and graded by size, create curved patterns, their contours emphasized by longer flint stones. Tepees of

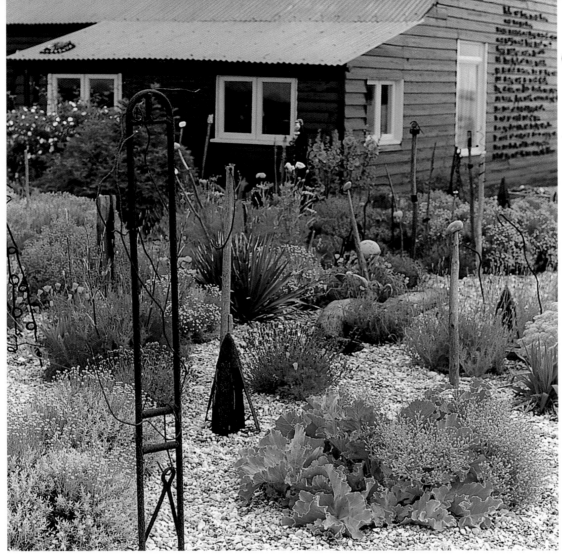

Left: Derek Jarman's pebble paradise of beachcombed driftwood and rusting metal with fennel, lavender, California poppies (Eschscholzia californica), and giant sea kale (Crambe maritima).

Below: More inspiration from the Chaumont garden festival, with jets and fountains of water tumbling over rocks, and boulders which are studded with curved patterns of small stones and pebbles.

Left: Wit and humor have a place in the garden, as is shown by this ingenious water display, featured as part of the annual Festival International des Jardins at the Château de Chaumont-sur-Loire.

beachcombed sticks, originally constructed to protect gorse cuttings from rabbits, and sea-weathered poles and planks used to support tender stems from the wind inspired a collection of natural sculptures that have survived the harshest winter winds. Using reclaimed railroad sleepers, Jarman constructed two raised beds, filled with imported soil, for growing herbs and vegetables. These beds also provided protection for a beehive, whose occupants feasted happily on the maritime flowers.

This wondrous place has the atmosphere of a Japanese meditational garden, combined with elements often found in English cottage gardens, and deliberately emphasizes the fragile relationship between a man-made and a natural environment. It also demonstrates how gardening presents a glorious opportunity to lose yourself and discover the pleasures of the outside world.

Color palette

Creating a harmonious balance of texture, form, and tone in an outside space relies on a sensitive choice of color. This can dramatically or subtly affect the mood and the ambience of the area. Pavings, walls, fences, ornaments, and furniture all contribute to the color in a garden.

Exterior paint and woodstain ranges, specially made to weather sun, rain, and frost, provide gardeners with a useful tool for creating permanent color. Introduced in this way, color can unify a garden design, add small touches of sharp contrast, or neutralize harsh surfaces. Although synthetic colors change endlessly according to the seasons, such permanent tones applied to walls and floors require more careful planning than more temporary accessories such as awnings or cushions.

Storyboard

Before making any decorating decision, interior designers generally compile a storyboard of colors and textures in roughly the proportion that they are likely to be used. They will often spot test a small area with a color before painting an entire room. Wood can be treated in the same way, but when staining exterior lumber, make sure that you know whether it is softwood or hardwood, as the finished results can be quite different in tone.

Many wood finishes combine a stain and varnish that flexes with the wood to prevent cracking or peeling. Sheds, trellis, and fences made from rough sawn lumber require a formula combined with preservative to prevent rot and inhibit mold growth. The advantage of choosing a woodstain is that it is absorbed into the lumber and allows the natural grain and character of the wood to show through.

floors &
walls

The two most important elements of any outside space are the floors and walls. Ground surfaces and boundaries must be well considered, for their size and proportion will define an area. They must be constructed with good solid foundations if they are to withstand inevitable changes in the ambient climate. These two features should complement each other and need to be planned together for the most successful results.

LEFT Shades of red are powerful and eye-catching and because of their "advancing" quality can make spaces appear smaller. Green is the complementary color of red and throws these stems into sharp contrast.

The ground, or floor, surface is the first element to consider when designing an outside space. Interior and garden designers always start with a basic floor plan, then divide the space and allocate specific areas to meet their clients' requirements.

In your garden you may want to create a terrace adjacent to the house, a raised bed for herbs, space for a shed, a water feature, or tall shrubs to screen an ugly building. Draw a plan of the space on graph paper, using a scale of 1:12, where each 1-in. (2.5-cm) square represents 1 ft. (30 cm), or a scale of 1:36, where each 1-in. (2.5-cm) square represents 1 yd. (90 cm). Mark all the existing elements accurately, and pencil in the proposed new features. Planning both interiors and gardens is similar to assembling a mosaic, in which everything is fitted together to form a harmonious living pattern. If you cut out pieces of paper scaled to the size of the new features, you can move them around your plan as you would furniture in a room. A floor plan will influence where and how to coordinate existing and new features, and allocating them space on paper will help you to determine the surface they require and how they are linked together.

Choosing a floor surface

The surface material for an outside space can be compared to the icing on a cake, but good quality and appropriate foundations are crucial. Try to be practical and realistic. You may fantasize about turning the whole space into a wildflower meadow, a wonderfully romantic project, but this will not be an option if you want a low-maintenance space. To turn an urban garden into a country paradise could involve removing all the topsoil and replacing it with grit, stones, and sand, all well dug in, then waiting several years to achieve your dream. Unless you have a huge area to play with, it is more practical to

Right: A polished wooden floor merges with the lumber decking, which accommodates a series of mature trees. This is a successful way to create a seamless link between the interior and its connecting outside space.

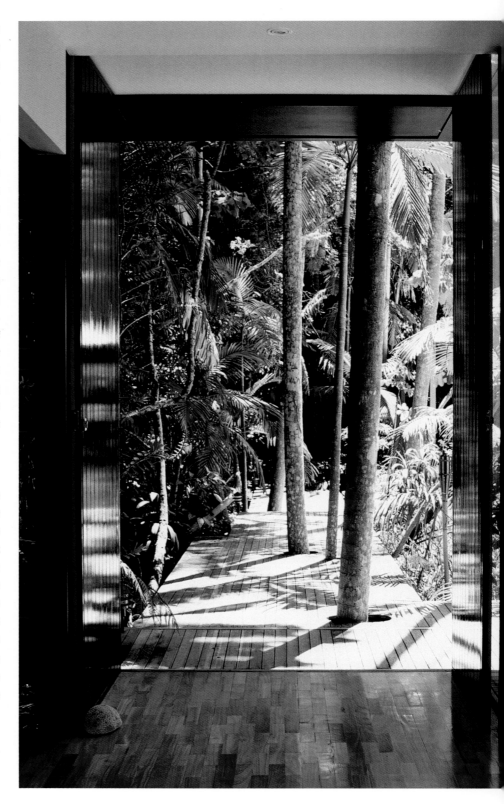

design a space for living that you can enjoy for the majority of the year and to minimize the stress involved in creating it.

Any outside floor should be well constructed if it is to be hardwearing and be able to withstand temperature changes. If it is to be laid on a balcony or roof, it needs to be watertight. The floor may also need to incorporate a drainage system and/or power cables for irrigation systems and lighting, and in sunrooms it could include underfloor heating.

The range of outside temperatures should influence your choice. In particular, roof terraces subjected to months of hot sun require a surface that will maintain a reasonably cool temperature, otherwise walking around with bare feet will be impossible. One of the joys of stepping outside is to be able to kick off your shoes and feel the fresh air. Lumber deck has long been one of the most popular surfaces in America. Like any wooden floor, a deck must be made of a suitable lumber and laid perfectly flat. It can be constructed like a false floor to make an outside space on the same level as the interior floor; unlike other flooring materials, wooden planks permit water to drain away. Besides creating a transition between house and garden, a deck will cover sloping or uneven ground and can conceal an old, worn-out patio. If there is a considerable drop between the interior and exterior, a raised deck will provide useful storage space underneath. There is a choice of suitable lumber including redwood, Western red cedar, and cypress. The less-expensive Southern yellow pine is both incredibly strong and environmentally sound. Reputable suppliers can provide pressure-treated and redried lumber, which is resistant to both rot and insect decay. It can be stained or left to weather naturally to a soft driftwood gray, which is compatible with brick, slate and stone.

In hot spots such as roof terraces and balconies, avoid a bright, white floor surface, as the intense light will reflect up into your eyes and make relaxing and reading uncomfortable. Softer, neutral, shades such as cream, taupe and buff blend easily

with brick and stone, and with soft landscaping. On a patio, balcony, or roof terrace, an effective scheme is to echo the color of the interior floor with the adjoining exterior.

Unless the ground is subject to extreme heat, solid floors of concrete, stone slabs, or bricks are the most practical adjacent to a building. The surfaces of halls and entrances always receive more wear than those in bedrooms, so just as you would choose a heavy-duty carpet or flooring on these areas, use hardwearing surfaces for outside entrances and exits. Unlike a wooden deck which can be laid completely flat next to a building because water drains between the planks, a solid floor requires a slope or a "fall" away from the house with a minimum gradient of 1:100 to prevent water puddling. In situ concrete, which is cast on site, can look very attractive when it is laid to a professional standard, and a dye or colored gravel can be added to make it look more interesting.

Above: This garden is infused with the soft, warm light of a sunset. The sheltering wall was painted in a dusky terra cotta and then decorated with a Moorish-style design which echoes the shapes of the surrounding trees.

Lawn versus gravel

A dilemma facing the owners of many small gardens is the lawn. If you inherit a grassy space, should you keep it? Remember that even a tiny piece of turf needs mowing, watering, and feeding, to keep it in good health. Then there is the equipment and where to store it. If you must have a lawn, give it a well-defined shape—formal, straight edges are more contemporary than undulating curves, although the latter provide areas for planting flowers and shrubs. It is well worth laying a mowing edge of bricks or paving which allows the lawnmower to run easily over the top. This edge gives the lawn good definition, protects plants in the borders, and avoids the necessity of hand-cutting the grass edges. Simple or intricate patterns based on circles or squares can be created with stone or concrete paving stones or bricks. Fill in the sections with small stones or gravel, or even plant them with neatly trimmed grass. A checkerboard pattern of bricks, filled in with gravel or planted with herbs such as chamomile (*Chamaemelum nobile Treneaguei*), Corsican mint (*Mentha requienni*), or creeping thyme (*Thymus serpyllum*), will release an aromatic scent when they are crushed underfoot.

Areas of gravel contained by brick or stone borders give a degree of flexibility to a garden. Gravel is fast replacing the urban lawn in popularity as a low-maintenance surface, which can include planting "pockets" for Mediterranean perennials that tolerate neglect if they are given a sunny spot and good drainage. One British gardener's inspirational gravel garden, created on a dry site previously used as a parking lot, is proof that lavender, rosemary, santolina, rue, and sage will flourish in these arid conditions. All these plants are strongly scented because the aromatic oils in their leaves help to conserve moisture and protect them from drought. In shady positions, gravel provides dry walkways between moisture-loving ferns and hostas.

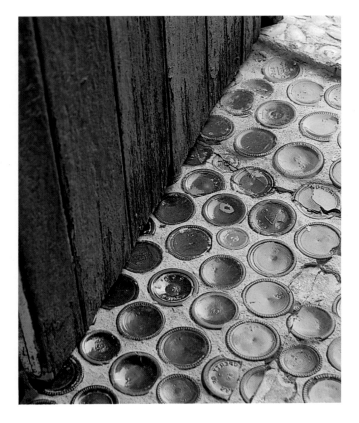

Raised beds add character to a space and serve as the equivalent of a huge container filled with the soil of your choice and planted accordingly. A raised bed increases the temperature of the soil, which does make it drier, but also protects vulnerable plants from the worst frost. Tall evergreen shrubs will provide year-round shade, shelter, and privacy; alternatively, the bed can be planted with fast-growing perennials such as yellow meadow rue (*Thalictrum speciosissimum*) or sweet fennel (*Foeniculum vulgare*). Both of these plants grow to a height of 6½ ft. (2 m) and create a semitransparent screen which will visually divide one part of the garden from another. Alternatively, you could create the same effect with annual climbers trained on ornamental supports such as bamboo tepees or metal, willow, or hazel obelisks. Most of the old-fashioned sweet peas (*Lathyrus odorata*) are sweetly perfumed (though they prefer cool zones), and scarlet runner beans (*Phaseolus coccineus*) will create lush foliage, and pretty flowers, followed by a crop of fresh beans at the end of the summer.

Above: Insets such as pebbles and inset tiles add vibrant color and texture. The bases of recycled bottles were pressed into a bed of cement while it was still soft, to create a blue reflective surface which is both cool and pleasant underfoot.

Below: Gravel, stones, and pebbles make an excellent mulch, helping to retain precious water and suppressing the growth of unwanted plants, and also making weeding unnecessary.

Creating different levels

You can add another dimension to your floor plan by including one or more changes of level. A sloping site may almost demand re-planning in order to make it more people-friendly. A continuous steep slope can be terraced, somewhat like the hills in Umbria, Italy, or those in southern France, where flat steps are cut into the mountainside for planting vines and olive trees. Low, broad terraces defined by low retaining walls and linked by steps paved in complementary materials will transform what may have been previously considered a "difficult" site. Cultivation on these flat plateaus is much easier and can even include a paved or graveled area for sitting and entertaining.

Even one change of level can transform an otherwise rather dreary space. A paved terrace in front of a house can be enclosed and sheltered by building a raised bed around its boundaries, linked to another part of the garden by a series of steps.

Above: A path of broken terra cotta pots adjoins a fragrant bank of lavender (Lavandula x intermedia abrialii). The pots are filled with purple Heliotrope (Heliotropium "Marine"), white Lantana camara and Helichrysum italicum.

Real and virtual walls

Room dividers such as open bookcases and shelving systems are used very effectively in studio apartments and loft spaces to differentiate one area from another, and the same technique can be applied outside with decorative trellis, panels of transparent glass blocks, arches, and pergolas. Horizontal and vertical surfaces are intrinsically linked in interior design, and they need to be considered together outdoors also.

A wall, fence, or boundary should always be chosen on its own merits and should look attractive without the embellishment of climbers or other planting. Foliage and flowers will soften the contours but they cannot replace quality materials and good construction. A boundary may need to be of a height and material to keep out intruders, or to create privacy, shelter, or shade. The most effective way to create an impenetrable wall is to plant evergreen barberry (*Berberidaceae*) or *Pyracantha*, both of which have virtually invisible but vicious thorns. A chain-link fence between posts secured in concrete bases will economically and effectively define a boundary and can be concealed in a couple of years with a wildlife hedge of bird, bee, and butterfly favourites such as European elder (*Sambucus nigra*), butterfly bush (*Buddleja davidii*), and hawthorn (*Crataegus monogyna*). Formal hedges of box (*Buxus sempervirens*), European hornbeam (*Carpinus betulus*), and English yew (*Taxus baccata*) are enjoying a revival, largely because electrically powered hedge-trimmers achieve in minutes what once took hours to cut by hand. To look their best, formal hedges need to be clipped in a slight taper, with the bottom wider than the top to allow air to circulate freely and so that light can reach all the branches. Less formal hedges of pruned lavender (*Lavandula*), rosemary (*Rosemarinus*), or the taller hazel (*Corylus avellana*) are also good "room dividers," separating one part of the garden from another. The rose *Rosa rugosa* makes an excellent fast-growing hedge with masses of small bristly thorns, heavily scented deep pink or white flowers, and large autumnal hips which make the best rose-hip syrup.

A new brick wall or fence may require some interesting texture or sympathetic coloring to blend it into its surroundings. An espaliered fruit tree grown against a brick or stucco south- or west-facing wall takes up little space and will thrive in these warm and sheltered positions. Ready-trained trees can be bought from specialist nurseries and, like conventional fruit trees, burst into pretty white blossom in spring, followed by lush foliage, and fruit in late summer. Even in winter, when the branches are bare, their shape forms a beautiful living sculpture. Espaliers need regular feeding and careful pruning twice a year, but they are an ideal way to grow fruit trees in a small space.

Left: Painted in subtle shades of blue, two stucco partition walls divide this garden and frame the view of a contemporary water feature. The wall-mounted pot overspills with water, which then trickles softly into the pond below.

Left: A slatted timber wall painted in deep terra cotta contrasts with the green foliage of an espaliered fruit tree and a cream picture frame, to make a simple but effective focal point.

Below: Wall and ground merge together, and interest is created by providing deliberate planting pockets for the contrast of spiky yucca and rosette-forming sempervivum.

Paint effects

Some walls and fences are much improved by paint or woodstain. Stucco walls present a perfect surface for painting, but it is important to use a product with a permeable finish; this allows any moisture trapped in the wall to escape, while still protecting the surface. You can create layers of color by adding painted wooden trellis in a contrasting shade or silvery wire panels. Stains are not just limited to wood tones, but are available in a rainbow of colors. Many contain a preservative and increase the longevity of the lumber, as well as softening the often harsh, rusty tones of new fencing. Different woods will take up color to varying degrees, so it is a good idea to test a small section, let it dry, and then inspect the color before staining an entire fence. If you cannot find your ideal color, try mixing two or three until you have achieved the desired effect.

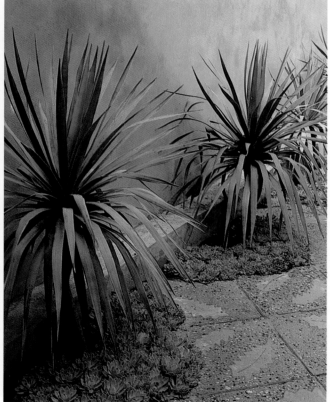

The walls of a dark basement area can benefit considerably from being painted a soft white or pale neutral tone. Panels of wooden or metal trellis will provide visual interest, either left bare or used to support shade-tolerant climbers. If the basement is sheltered and frost-free, there are numerous tropical plants (more commonly sold as houseplants) that tolerate a warm and shady outside habitat. Another possibility is to securely attach shelves to the walls with metal brackets and to grow pots of trailing plants such as ivies or cascading ferns. In the tiny courtyards and patios of Andalucia in Spain, vertical surfaces are crammed with pots slotted into metal rings affixed to walls, or hung from guttering or pipes. In this fiercely hot climate the predominant plant is *pelargonium*, which thrives in a minimum of poor soil and flowers profusely for most of the year. Wholesale copying of this style is really successful only if you can provide the same vibrant Spanish sunlight and brilliant blue skies, but the principle of covering your patio wall with hundreds of pots can be stunning. Stick to one color for the pots and be prepared to spend hours watering, especially if you decide to clad the wall of a roof terrace in this manner.

Right: A wall painted blue provides the foundation for the trellis supporting wisteria on this sunny terrace. Indian saris are suspended between the trellis and the adjoining house to make a colorful shady canopy.

Above: A curved transparent panel extending up from the brick wall creates distorted and abstract reflections of the trees and plants in the foreground.

Right: A wall of multi-layered foliage provides a tiny wooden-decked backyard with shade and privacy. Within the fronds of the ground cover ferns are the luminous white flowers of impatiens walleriana.

High-rise walls

The climate on a roof or balcony is different from that on the ground. For one thing, summer heat is usually more intense; but the main factor is the wind, which can dry out pots, cause leaf-burn to foliage, and create an uncomfortable environment for people. Rooftop walls need to filter the power of the wind, rather than trying to block it entirely, which causes turbulence. Sturdy trellis performs the job perfectly and is available as preformed panels or as custom-built fences of stout bamboo canes or lightweight metal mesh.

In some parts of Europe, wattle fencing made from woven willow branches is a traditional method for creating solid-looking but wind-permeable walls. A bamboo pole screen will also provide an attractive framework, in front of which climbing plants can be grown in containers. You can also improvise an

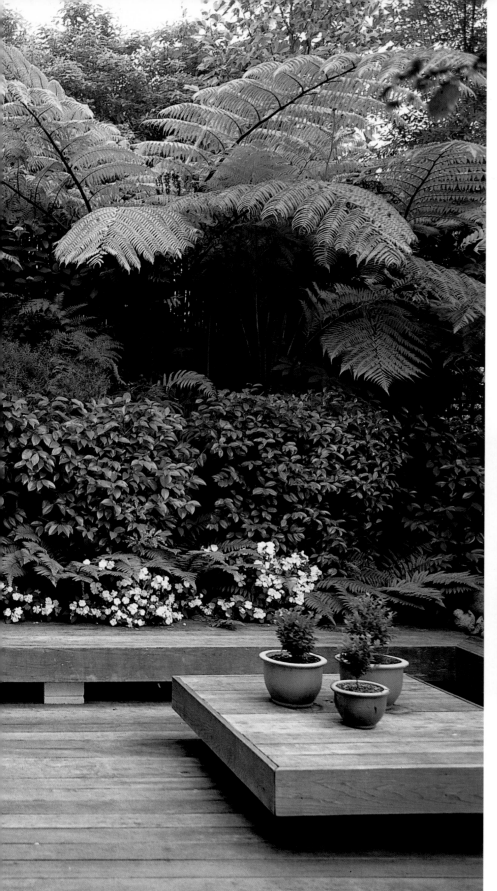

extra filter out of green mesh netting, sold in garden centers to protect fruit bush from birds. Once fixed on the outside of the screen, it is virtually undetectable from the inside and ensures protection for the plants on the terrace.

If space and weight-loading permit, you could grow a completely natural windbreak by creating a hedge of conifer. The dwarf cultivars of Western red cedar (*Thuja plicata*) can easily be controlled by annual clipping, and the leaves and small branches release a wonderful pineapple-like aroma when crushed. On urban rooftops where a terrace is protected by the close proximity of taller buildings, a wall of gently rustling bamboo will provide shelter, shade, and privacy.

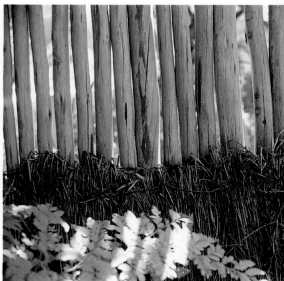

Above: Texture can add vital interest to repetitive vertical surfaces. This is clearly demonstrated with these bleached wooden poles, which are combined with a dense screen of rough twigs which are woven together with fine wire.

PAINTED BRICK WALL

For the reluctant gardener, paint is a very effective way to introduce color in an outside space. Wooden furniture, fencing, trellis, plant stands, and containers can all be painted to harmonize or contrast with their surroundings. Blue is particularly successful with natural greens, enhancing the color of foliage instead of competing with it. Choose the luminous bold shades found in Mediterranean and Caribbean climates, or the cooler tones used in northern countries where the light is softer.

Water-based masonry paint is available in ready-mixed colors, which will provide years of protection. Other colors can be mixed by specialist paint suppliers. If the wall is still powdery after cleaning with a stiff brush, it may need a coat of primer-sealer to seal the surface before painting.

If you are decorating a large wall, it is wise to paint a small area first and observe the result at different times of the day before painting the rest. It's astonishing how colors change with the light.

MATERIALS AND EQUIPMENT

- plastic sheeting

- wire brush

- large latex paintbrush

- deep blue latex masonry paint

- plastic or rubber lizards

- waterproof adhesive

- small can of metallic-finish car touch-up paint (optional)

- small artist's paintbrush (optional)

- mussel shells, washed and well scrubbed

1 Protect the ground at the base of the wall with plastic sheeting. Remove loose dirt or flaking paint with a wire brush. Do not worry about gaps between the bricks, as these will be filled with paint, and an uneven texture is expected on an exterior wall.

2 A special latex brush gives the best results with water-based paints. Apply the paint generously, filling all the gaps and holes. Leave to dry completely.

GARDEN DECORATOR

Left: Plastic or rubber lizards such as these can be found at toy shops.

3 Attach the lizards to the wall with waterproof adhesive, so that they appear to be running up it. If the lizards' skin coloring is too crude, alter it with car touch-up paint, using a small paintbrush.

4 Finally, apply a thick mulch of mussel shells to cover the bare earth at the foot of the wall with a layer of darker blue.

SLATE WITH WOODEN STEPPING "STONES"

This design was inspired by the peaceful serenity of Japanese gravel gardens. The wooden blocks appear to float on a sea of slate which links a small courtyard to a raised garden beyond. The contrast of color and texture is pleasing, and this is an ideal way to cover precast concrete paving. One of the attractions of slate is that it changes color from gleaming dark gray, when wet, to a pale, light-reflective tone when dry. The slate acts like a mulch, and rainwater will soak through the stones and drain away, so fit any outside drain with a grill, using a mesh fine enough to prevent any stones from causing a blockage.

The wooden blocks are freestanding, so they must be heavy enough to walk on safely. Arranged in a path, they lead the eye to discover the more secluded part of the garden beyond. Even small gardens can be divided into distinct spaces, each with its own character.

1 For this path, the wood blocks for the stepping-stones were made from three decking planks cut and screwed at right angles to two other planks. Place the stepping-stones in position before surrounding them with a shallow mulch of slate chips or gravel.

Left: The lower part of each wooden block should be surrounded by slate, to create a natural effect.

MATERIALS AND TOOLS

- pretreated wood blocks, each approximately 10 in. (25 cm) square and 2½ in. (6 cm) thick

- slate chips or other coarse gravel

- large clam shells

Left: The simplest solution is often the most effective. With very little effort, a character-less area of concrete paving can be transformed into crisp and contemporary flooring.

Below: If the slate is laid thinly on a hard concrete surface, space can be cleared for chairs and tables to stand quite safely.

2 As a relief to the formal, horizontal line of the path, you may want to add some rounded shapes. Here, four terra cotta pots, planted with round box shapes, are defined with circles of clam shells

VARIATION

Even pretreated wood can be colored using an exterior woodstain. Choose a color to complement the foliage and contrast with the gray slate.

furniture & furnishings

Relaxation is often one of the main attractions of a garden—it should be a place where you can enjoy the fresh air in peace and privacy. When choosing furniture and furnishings for an outside space, you might like to include a comfortable bench, nestling between aromatic shrubs chosen for their evening scent, or a generous-sized table where you can sit and enjoy a summer lunch with family and friends. Comfort and practicality are key elements here. And remember that simple designs and natural materials will complement any setting.

LEFT The elegantly shaped and perfectly proportioned metal chairs shown here have an eye-catching, sculptural quality. They also serve a dual practical purpose—either for sitting on or for displaying plants.

Above: Built into the walls of a sheltered balcony, this versatile cushioned banquette is long enough to lie on. With the addition of a low table it would also provide a dining space for two or three people.

However you have designed your garden, there will be times when all you really want to do is just sit out there and relax. This is when you discover whether you have created a place for people, or a showcase for plants and objects.

Finding the right position for a "living room" contributes considerably to outdoor comfort, so at the initial stage, mark areas on your plan that are warm and sheltered, ideally offering privacy and with a pleasing outlook.

All the senses must be satisfied in order to achieve a state of complete relaxation. The pleasure of smell is very important out of doors—fresh air has a fantastic scent of its own which is enhanced by aromatic herbs such as rosemary and lavender, or sweetly perfumed jasmine and roses. Scented flowers create a wonderfully relaxing ambience, particularly in the evening, when their fragrance is more intense. An attractive view of green plants and flowers appeals to our sense of sight, and the sounds of water and birdsong are very soothing to our ears. And hard surfaces of stone or metal can be covered with fat, squashy cushions to make them comfortable.

Alfresco dining

Sensitive positioning is as important as your choice of furniture. A raised brick flowerbed can be designed to incorporate a bench seat with the dimensions of a generous sofa, surrounded by scented flowers and shrubs. Constructed along one side of a paved patio, this should be long enough to lie on or to provide seating for three or four people with the support of a well-padded seat and back cushions. Add a rectangular table and free-standing chairs and you can easily accommodate eight or nine people. This dining area needs at least 3½sq. yards (3sq. meters) of floor space to give freedom of movement and easy access. If this is impossible, you could have a freestanding bench instead of chairs, ideally placed against a wall so that diners have back support. Some outdoor chairs are very lightweight, and for these, the ground underneath needs to be perfectly flat, or they will always have an irritating wobble when you sit on them. However, lightweight portable chairs are space-saving, as they fold flat or stack neatly.

Where a terrace is adjacent to the kitchen or dining room and on the same level, a dining table with lockable casters could double up for both inside and outside. A weatherproof table that can be left permanently outside may provide a useful place for planted containers, especially in the winter, when it is unlikely to be used for dining. A table is also the ideal height for a potting bench. Stone mosaic table tops in vibrant glazed patterns look decorative on a paved terrace, while an unglazed, muted design would blend into the hard landscaping. Marble, limestone, and slate make elegant, hard-wearing table tops which withstand any degree of heat or cold from the natural elements and require little maintenance. These materials are perfect for dining, as they are unaffected by squashed fruit or spilled salad dressing.

Left: Delicate detailing makes this metal bench as much a decorative object as a practical seat. Its removable cushions blend with the sunbaked colors of this Mediterranean courtyard.

Materials matter

One of the pleasures of alfresco eating is being oblivious of time passing, and this can be achieved only if the seating is comfortable and the dining space sheltered. An outside temperature that seems ideal when you are walking around or working can feel distinctly chilly if you are sitting still. Similarly, oppressively hot sun becomes pleasantly warm when it is filtered or partially blocked. A building or tree canopy may already create shade in your outdoor space, but if not, you can construct an artificial ceiling by rigging up a simple canvas canopy, supported by sturdy wooden or metal poles secured in concrete blocks or directly into the ground. Many outdoor tables have a central hole for a parasol secured with a weighted base. A more elaborate idea is a tubular steel or galvanized metal structure built over and above a permanent seat, which can be transformed into a leafy arbor with

roses, clematis, or other quick-growing climbers. Alternatively, canvas panels can be tied to the structure to create a temporary shelter from wind and sun. On a small patio surrounded by solid walls, you may be able to fix metal hooks from which to run metal wires, as on some drapery rods, and from these you can attach lengths of canvas or cheaper unbleached muslin with metal clips.

On an upper terrace or roof garden, extra protection may be required to compensate for the more exposed position. The strongest part of a roof is around its perimeter, and here you can construct wooden seating, combined with planters and protected by a screen of trellis or another semipermeable "wall." Garden storage can be incorporated under the seat for pots and tools, barbecue charcoal, and bags of potting mixture. The base could also be designed to be removed entirely or hinged to a frame. This type of seating is perma-

Below: These concrete benches make permanent and maintenance-free seating. They are subtly decorated with inlaid ceramic tiles—the design echoes the same random pattern of the brick floor.

tile, ranging from simply styled French café chairs and tables to more intricately patterned Victorian wrought iron benches. The disadvantage of wrought iron is the cost, particularly for original designs, and also the weight. One advantage of lightweight chairs is that they can be shifted to follow the sun and quickly brought inside if the weather changes.

Many interior furniture designs have been adapted for outside use but have come back indoors in response to the need for lightweight folding chairs in small homes and studios. In interiors where storage space is limited, some furniture can be used both inside and out. Flat-folding canvas and wood director's chairs with removable seats and backs are comfortable as well as appropriate to the setting. With different sets of canvas covers, these chairs can be adapted to match any color scheme, and because they fold flat are easily transported.

Below: These crisp white painted metal French café chairs and the simple folding table are classic designs for indoors and out. They stack flat and such furniture is ideal for smaller homes where space for storage is at a premium.

Above: Subtly concealed from obvious view and surrounded by a wall-trained fig and a towering Agapanthus "Snowy owl," this is a perfect place for a time of quiet seclusion in the soft evening light.

nent and therefore needs to be weatherproof. In parts of Europe, teak has long been a popular choice for outdoor seating, although concern about the depletion of the rainforest has led to the use of other woods. In the United States, cedar and redwoods are especially valued for their beauty and natural resistance to insect damage and decay, but they are expensive, as are other rot-resistant woods, including black locust and red mulberry. Less costly lumber, such as pine, can be made resistant to rot and insects by impregnation with various chemicals, including chromated copper arsenate (CCA) and ammoniacal copper quat (ACQ). Such treated woods can be oiled, stained, or painted; however, outdoor furniture made from these timbers may need a fresh coat of wood preservative each year to prevent rotting.

Metal will also succumb to the weathering effects of sun and rain. Distressed surfaces can be attractive, but the hinges of metal tables and chairs should be protected from rusting and oiled regularly to keep them in good working order. Painted metal furniture is immensely functional and versa-

Total relaxation

Many outdoor chairs are perfect for sitting at a table, but a more comfortable, reclining chair is needed for serious relaxation. There are scores of designs developed from the original deck chairs, created for luxury liners. Rows of these reclining wooden seats with adjustable, elongated leg rests are provided to enable passengers to enjoy the view of the ocean and breathe the clean, salty air. In the days when passenger ships plied regularly across the Atlantic, people used them even in winter, muffled in warm blankets. Many contemporary adaptations of this classic design are made from hollow metal tube frames with plastic or metal mesh covers. These new versions of the deck chair are designed to be lightweight and easy to carry. Looks are only one factor, so apply the same comfort requirements as you would when choosing a bed. You need to be able to stretch out totally and to feel supported in the middle of your back.

Perhaps the cheapest and most popular version of the lounger is the good old-fashioned adjustable wood-framed garden chair, with its canvas sling seat. Its simple design can be seen on beaches and in parks all over the world. It is still very practical for small outside spaces, and newer models are designed so the canvas seat is easy to remove, to be stored somewhere clean and dry when not in use. This chair also has the curious ability to look at home in any outdoor setting, be it a formal traditional garden or an ultra-modern terrace. The original versions have a wooden frame, but there are now modern designs made of lightweight tubular aluminum frames covered with tough woven synthetic fabrics, and some even have a rocking mechanism. The modern "butterfly" chair consists of a canvas bucket-shaped seat slung onto a wire frame, which folds into a neat bundle; the covers can be removed for storage and the occasional machine wash. In a minimalist outside space, with restrained planting and large areas of concrete or stone, these chairs, judiciously placed, have a pleasing sculptural appearance.

Left: In traditional gardens it is the flowers and plants that introduce color to the overall design. However, in this contemporary outside room, the trees are used for their sculptural quality, and it is the lemon and orange canvas butterfly chairs that exude vibrant color and contrast invitingly with the deep purple perimeter wall.

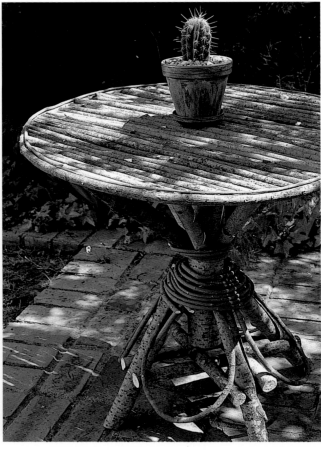

Modern classics

The updated versions of café-style tables and chairs that have replaced slatted wooden furniture are often coated in a hardwearing, water-resistant resin, subtly colored in contemporary colors such as aqua, pistachio, and lime. Even classically styled metal or wooden benches can be adapted to suit modern surroundings. The designer and architect Sir Edwin Lutyens created elegant furniture for many of the famous gardens he designed in collaboration with Gertrude Jekyll, and with its perfect proportions, it still has a place in today's outdoor spaces.

Natural wood furniture blends with foliage and flowers, but if painted or stained a bright cobalt blue or deep Etruscan red, it becomes a strong focal point, particularly in winter, when there is little other color in the garden. Sympathetic colors can also be applied to other wooden structures such as trellis and planters. One idea is to link the furniture with the detailing of the trellis by repeating the same chinoiserie or lattice pattern on the seat backs.

Less conventional furniture can be instantly created with a wide, splinter-free plank spanned across two logs or piles of bricks. Positioned against a sheltered, east-facing wall, this is the perfect place to enjoy early-morning sunshine. For resting at the end of a summer day, nothing beats a hammock. There are modern designs with swing seats on frames, but the simplest version is canvas or a similar fabric sling-tied at two points with rope. Strong supports are, of course, essential, and this could be by means of metal hooks driven into brick walls or, more traditionally, rope firmly secured around the trunks of mature, healthy trees.

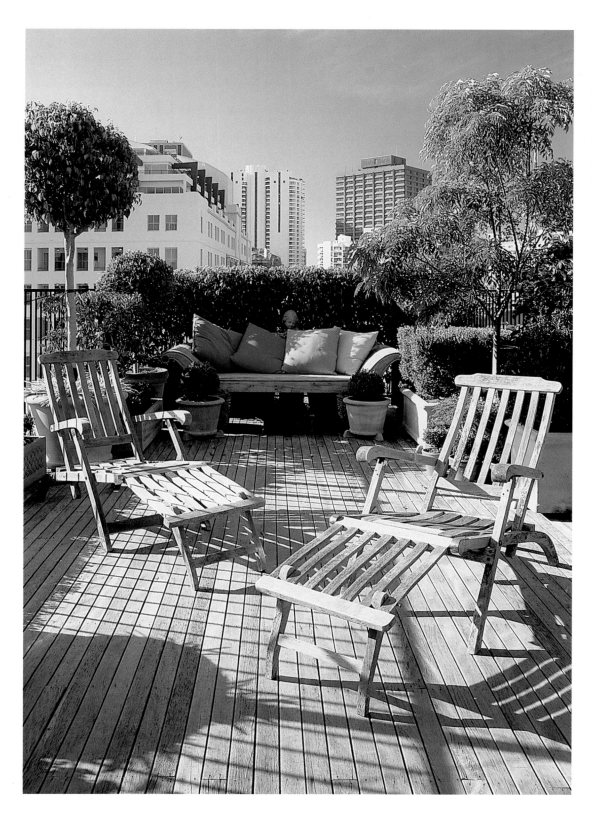

Left: Deck chairs—
reclining wooden seats
with adjustable leg
rests—have long graced
the decks of luxury
liners. Here, they look
equally at home on
this wooden-decked
roof terrace.

CHAIR COVERS

Café-style chairs are very popular, as they are lightweight, can be stored flat, and, being constructed from metal and wood, are reasonably weatherproof. To make them more comfortable, add simple seat covers filled with foam pillow forms and slip-over back covers containing a thin layer of foam padding. Use the same fabric in various colors to make a coordinated set of mix-and-match covers.

MATERIALS AND EQUIPMENT

- brown paper
- pre-cut foam pillow form
- washable fabric in contrasting colors
- dressmaker's pins
- thin foam sheet
- matching sewing threads
- 2 snap fasteners or 1 zipper for each chair seat
- colored woven tape
- sewing machine

1 To make the seat covers, cut a brown paper pattern of the pre-cut foam pad, allowing an extra 1½ in. (4 cm) seam allowance all around, depending on the thickness of the pad. Using this as a pattern, cut out two pieces of fabric for each chair.

2 Pin two contrasting fabric pieces together with right sides facing. Machine-stitch around the edge, leaving an opening large enough to insert the pad. Hem both sides of the opening and add two snaps or a zipper.

3 Turn the cushion covers right side out. Stitch a length of woven tape on each side for tying the cushions to the chair frames.

4 To make the back cushions, it is important to measure each chair individually. Cut a piece of fabric the width of the chair back plus ½ in. (1 cm) seam allowance on both sides, and 1½ times the length of the seat back plus ½ in. (1 cm) seam allowance. Fold back the extra half-length and turn over 1 in. (2.5 cm) to make a hem. This pocket will hold the foam when the cushion is on the chair.

5 Cut a piece of contrasting fabric the width of the chair plus ½ in. (1 cm) seam allowance on both sides, and the length of the seat back plus an extra 1 in. (2.5 cm) to make a hem. Pin the two pieces together, right sides facing, adjusting if necessary until they match exactly. Machine-stitch the top and sides. Cut a piece of thin foam to fit the cover, and insert it in the pocket. Turn the cover right side out.

VARIATION

As a variation, you can add a second pocket to the back cushion for storing an individual place setting and napkin. Stitch this extra pocket onto the fabric before pinning the sides together.

TILED TRAY TABLE

Many softwood furniture designs intended for use indoors can be customized and weatherproofed for the garden, and a low butler's-tray table makes an ideal surface for serving food and drinks. The table is painted with an exterior finish, then covered with a loose layer of ceramic tiles to provide a heatproof surface and to give it extra weight for added stability. Odd tiles can be bought very cheaply at home centers and tile specialists, but they must all be the same size and thickness. The frame folds flat, and the tiles are removable, so the table can be moved indoors in the winter.

MATERIALS AND EQUIPMENT

- sandpaper
- damp cloth
- medium-size paintbrush
- water-based undercoat
- colored exterior paint
- ceramic tiles
- tile-cutter (optional)

1 Lightly sand the surface of the table to give a good tooth for the undercoat.

2 Wipe down with a damp cloth to remove any dust. Paint the entire tray and frame with undercoat, taking care not to leave any gaps that could allow water to penetrate the finish. Leave to dry completely, then apply a coat of exterior paint.

3 You will probably not find tiles that will exactly fit the tray, so some will need to be cut with a tile-cutter. Alternatively, tiles can be professionally cut, a service offered by many tile dealers.

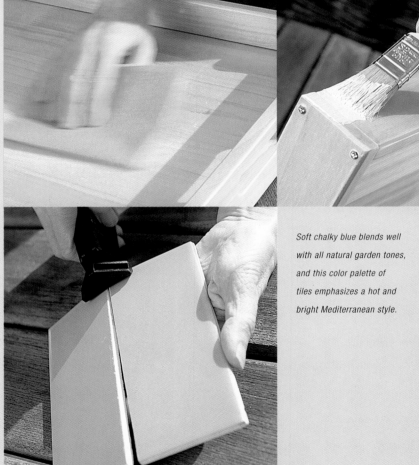

Soft chalky blue blends well with all natural garden tones, and this color palette of tiles emphasizes a hot and bright Mediterranean style.

4 Arrange the tiles in a decorative pattern. As they are only loosely laid, they can easily be rearranged.

5 If the tray, or any softwood furniture, is intended to be used on a lawn, screw a rubber stop to the bottom of each leg to prevent damp from penetrating the paintwork.

BURLAP CUSHIONS

Certain fabrics are traditionally associated with outside living——canvas or sailcloth are used for sturdy awnings and canopies, and washable plastic or plasticized cotton makes practical tablecloths. Roughly-woven burlap is ideal for outdoor cushion covers, as it is hard-wearing and inexpensive. The natural pale biscuit color coordinates well with stone and cement seats, and it also dyes well. Colors such as eggplant, terra cotta, inky blue, or any shade of leaf green look good outdoors. Washing-machine dye is colorfast and will not permanently stain the machine. Each cushion cover will shrink approximately 2 in. (5 cm) in each direction all round during the dyeing, so it is important to allow for this when you are cutting out the fabric.

MATERIALS AND EQUIPMENT

- scissors
- fine burlap
- pillowforms
- dressmaker's pins
- washing-machine dye
- salt for each package of dye (see manufacturer's instructions)
- powdered detergent
- fabric conditioner
- embroidery thread, in a contrasting color
- embroidery needle
- matching sewing thread
- sewing machine

1 Cut a piece of burlap 2 in. (5 cm) in both directions larger than the pillow. Fold under 1 in. (2.5 cm) along one of the short ends, pin in place and machine stitch. Repeat at the other short end, but this time fold it over again to make a neat hem, and topstitch. Fold over this neat hem to a depth of 6 in. (15 cm) and stitch both sides of the flap. Fold the burlap in half, with the flap on the outside, and machine stitch down both long sides. Turn the cover inside out. Make as many more covers as you need in the same way.

Left: Soften the hard contours of a solid wooden bench with several burlap pillows, dyed to blend with the surrounding colors of the garden.

2 Machine-wash the burlap covers before dyeing to remove any oils that may affect the process. Machine-wash them again with the dye and salt, following the manufacturer's instructions. Finally, machine-wash the covers once again, using detergent and a generous amount of fabric conditioner to improve the feel of the burlap.

3 Using an embroidery needle and contrasting embroidery thread, hand-sew a decorative blanket stitch border along all four sides of each cushion cover. Insert the pillowforms into the covers.

59

features & focal points

Every outside space should have at least one intriguing feature that makes an impression. A terrace may have a stunning view; one garden may contain a secluded area of peace and privacy; another may include one spectacular tree, or a pergola resplendent with the chandelier-shaped flowers of fragrant wisteria. Features and focal points may be temporary delights or have a degree of seasonal change which continually refreshes their visual impact.

LEFT   Natural sculpture like this weather-worn lumber and these sea-washed pebbles and shells have a simple Zen-like quality. The simple positioning of every feature shows absolute attention to detail.

Above: A formal gravel garden defined by stone edging makes a contrast in color and texture to the surrounding soft landscaping and has great impact when viewed from above.

Nearly every element in an outside space can be given some distinctive decorative quality to make it into a stunning feature. A stucco wall painted in a strong color will arrest the eye and make a sharp contrast with its surroundings. An intricately patterned design of gravel, pebbles, paving, and plants is a practical way of combining form and function with decoration. A rose-covered arbor seat offers a profusion of color and scent in summer, and creates a shady retreat that is sheltered and private. A simple tepee of bamboo, or a distressed metal obelisk, may be deemed a garden sculpture, while at the same time providing a self-supporting structure for scarlet runner beans or sweet peas. These structures can also look very dramatic in winter, when their naked frames are covered with snow or a sharp frost.

Trees and plants

A single striking object may be all that is required to create dramatic interest, even in the smallest of spaces. A tiny garden could benefit from one beautiful tree or large plant. Tree ferns (*Dicksonia antarctica*), natives of the temperate rainforests of Australasia, are hardy in mild, sheltered areas, prefer shade and need protection from winds. They are ideal for urban gardens, and because they do not have any roots but receive all their moisture and nutrients from their fronds and upper trunk, they grow quite happily in containers. A mature specimen will stand some 33 ft. (10 m) tall and its fronds can be 10 ft. (3 m) long.

Architectural-looking plants suitable for sunrooms and warm zones include the Chusan palm (*Trachycarpus fortunei*) and the dwarf palm

Right: This well-established tree is encircled with a seat of fencing made from woven willow and a place to sit and enjoy the view of the landscape beyond the garden.

(*Chamaerops humilis*). The dwarf palm is a European native and reaches a height of about 10 ft. (3 m), half the size of the Chusan palm. Tree ferns and palms grow slowly, so purchasing a mature specimen is a major investment; but they are living sculptures and will be an elegant, space-saving feature on a small terrace or in a garden room.

Containers are ideal for bamboos, as this kind of planting will restrain the invasive habits of many of this species. With rustling leaves which are often strikingly variegated, and colored stems varying from golden yellow to inky black, bamboos thrive in shelter and shade. Grown individually in simple pots or metal containers, they bring a feeling of peacefulness to modern spaces, and their reedlike stems have a natural affinity with water. Grown en masse, bamboos create a dramatic jungle through which paths can be cut and clearings made—a private paradise hidden from the outside world. Unlike palms, some varieties of bamboo will withstand temperatures well below 68° F (20° C), which makes them a fine evergreen feature in winter.

It is in winter that outside spaces can truly be assessed for the quality of their "bone structure," and for a tree to earn the status of an ornamental feature it needs to have all-year-round interest. Trees should be assessed for their shape, bark, flowers, and fruit; for unlike non-organic ornaments, trees will change in color and form over the seasons. Specialty nurseries can give advice and supply suitable trees, priced according to maturity and size. Numerous varieties of Japanese maple (*Acer palmatum*), ornamental cherry (*Prunus*), and pear (*Pyrus calleryana* "Bradford") make an attractive central focus in a graveled courtyard or a planting pocket in paving. It is often recommended to plant these trees in late October, but they have been successfully planted as early as August, when the soil is a little warmer.

Vertical structures

Pergolas, archways, and tunnels are usually associated with country gardens, but these shapes are also invaluable in making the best use of limited space in an urban setting. Creating a false ceiling and dividing an area can actually make it appear larger than it really is.

Just as a change of level adds horizontal interest to even the tiniest garden or patio, so too an arch of woven willow can be used to designate one "room" from another. In winter, the bare brown branches have a sculptural quality, and with careful planting they can be covered with an early-flowering clematis followed by another variety that blooms in summer or fall. Freshly planted willow stems also take root quickly and will burst into leaf in the spring.

Treated rustic poles or roughly sawn timbers blend well into natural or wildlife gardens, while plastered pillars and simply styled metalwork are better suited to modern or formal spaces. Metal arches and pergolas can be used with great effect to link a building with a garden or patio. Wooden or metal beams can be supported between a house and a freestanding pole or timber upright by means of joist hangers, to create a veranda. This offers semi-shade, and privacy from upstairs windows and adjoining properties. This style of structure is very common in southern France and in Italy, where the fronts of many houses are shaded from the sun and sheltered from wind and rain.

Whether attached to a building or freestanding, a veranda must be constructed with appropriate materials and firm foundations, particularly if it will be covered with perennial climbers. Many climbing plants grow at an amazing rate, and their sheer weight can make flimsy structures collapse unless the supports are sunk into concrete or specially designed metal spikes, which will protect them from contact with the wet soil. It is also important to ensure that the overhead structure is high enough to accommodate foliage such as the low-hanging flowers of wisteria or laburnum.

Features from the past

Many old houses are furnished and decorated with a reference to the past, often to the period when they were first built. Architectural details such as fireplaces are often retained and incorporated into the design scheme, even though their relevance has been superseded by central heating. In these homes it may be desirable to continue this style with formal, traditional outside spaces featuring eighteenth-century Italian-style balconies and balustrades and ornate metalwork furniture, arches, and screens in the spirit of the great French châteaus. Geometry, proportion, and perfect symmetry are features that are typical of this style, so the look can be created quite simply by placing classically styled urns, either in pairs or singly, at the center of a paved area, surrounded by an immaculate clipped boxwood hedge.

Sundials are a traditional form of exterior decoration dating back some 5,000 years. They tell only local time so, unless you have one made for you, an old sundial will probably be purely decorative. Other garden antiques, such as terra cotta rhubarb forcers, French glass cloches, or maraîchères (used to protect tender seedlings), or Victorian watering cans, appeal to those with an interest in the past. They all offer authentic traditional garden decoration and may serve to prompt the beginning of an addiction to collecting.

Huge pots and urns are very versatile garden ornaments. Standing alone, they give sculptural relief in the midst of lush planting or in isolation at the end of a path. They may be capacious enough to hold a small tree or to be filled with stones or sand an as effective foundation for anchoring a pole to support an awning or canopy. The most humble of terra cotta pots becomes a work of personal expression when painted or covered with a mosaic of broken china or seashells pressed into cement. Beachcombing for shells and small stones with holes will also provide natural ingredients for a hanging mobile or wind chime, strung together with garden twine or transparent fishing line.

Disguising the utilities

Some garden objects are dull or even plain ugly, and they need a decorative treatment that is more of a disguise than a focus. Sheds, gas and oil tanks, trashcans, compost piles, and even drainpipes, do not have to be eyesores.

Unless your garage is very spacious, a separate tool shed or workroom is essential to provide storage space for tools, furniture, pots, and equipment. Tools can be hung on wall racks, furniture stashed in simple frames attached to the ceiling, and rows of shelves can be provided for pots and equipment. Fertilizers and chemicals have to be stored carefully, so make sure that the lids are tightly closed and that they are placed well out of the reach of children and animals.

If you are buying a readymade tool shed it may be practical to choose something capacious and decorative, which could be used as a summer-house as well as for storage. A well-constructed, insulated garden room is particularly appealing to people who run a business from home, but need the psychological transition of leaving home to start work each day. Assuming that such a profession requires little more than chair and desk space, a summerhouse or shed with at least one window can be customized into a small but perfectly adequate workroom. Power for lighting, heat, and equipment can be connected to the main building. It should be installed by a qualified electrician to ensure that all the safety precautions are observed. Outside, wood paint or stain will quickly transform the exterior, and

Above: This raised wooden deck creates a warm sun trap between house and garden. The deck is subtly blended by painting the walls, deck joists, and furniture all the same color.

Right: Pennisetum villosum, *with its ethereal drooping flowerheads moving in the slightest breeze and contrasting effectively with the static sculptures of rounded stones which are held erect on silvery metal spikes.*

Below: A simple but effective idea. Recycled blue bottles pushed onto the spiked tops of a weather-worn fence glitter in the sun, forming a colorful and decorative border and attractively soften the fence's contours.

the building will blend into its surroundings if you attach trellis or wire supports to the sides and grow evergreen climbers or wall shrubs. A thick blanket of foliage will hide the shed and will also provide extra insulation.

Similar techniques can be applied to other vital but unattractive utilities such as trashcans and tanks. Enclose them with trellis or fencing, covered with climbers as further decorative camouflage. Alternatively, plant an evergreen hedge of common holly (*Ilex aquifolium*), bamboo, or yew (*Taxus baccata*). Almost any woody shrub, evergreen or deciduous, that produces strong secondary growth from its cut stems is suitable for hedging.

Garden furniture can sometimes be adapted to create hidden storage for unsightly objects—a huge pot can serve as a container for smaller pots or a hose; an old beehive can be converted into a bin

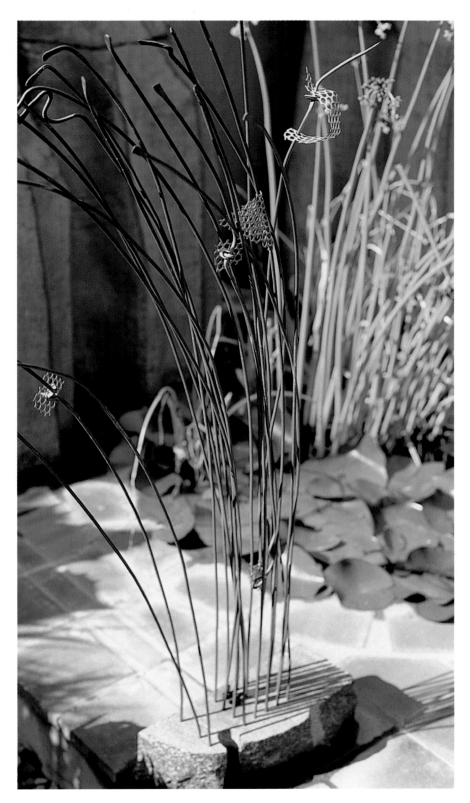

for compost or a garden store cupboard; and a garden seat could be constructed around a box with a hinged lid. The exterior of an old building is sometimes blighted with pipework, but fast-growing climbers such as ivies, many vines, wisteria, and clematis will cover the offending items in a few years. Some climbers appreciate wire supports, but many are self-clinging, and unless the property is extremely old, with crumbling mortar, they will do no harm to the masonry.

Outdoor art

Any purely decorative object you decide to include in your outdoor space will be determined by your personal taste and style. Many artists and sculptors now specialize in garden ornaments, and art and craft galleries increasingly exhibit their work.

Instead of a simple bench, a garden seat could be a unique piece created by a designer-maker to be functional as well as aesthetically pleasing. Artists such as Andy Goldsworthy, in England, have inspired others to work with natural materials; Goldsworthy's influence on modern garden culture encourages us to look at leaves, twigs, and stones in a very different light. Garden ornaments such as birds and animals fashioned from wire or reclaimed materials can be witty and amusing but still have integrity. Traditional topiary figures were laboriously fashioned by clipping box or yew, but readymade frames in the shapes of animals or simple cones, spheres, and spirals have given us a shortcut to creating designs out of ivy or clematis. One step further is to introduce living ornaments such as exotic breeds of chicken or fish. In large country gardens, geese were traditionally kept to scare off intruders, but a smaller garden may be able to accommodate a pair of tame ducks, which will organically keep the slug population in check.

Left: This contemporary sculpture exactly captures the effect of tall reeds and arching grasses. It would make an ideal permanent focal point of a small pond or a modern water feature.

PAINTED BIRDHOUSE

MATERIALS AND EQUIPMENT

- tape measure

- soft pencil

- old floorboard approximately 1 yd. (1m) long

- set square

- saw

- drill, with hole-cutter attachment

- 4 in. (10 cm) piece of doweling

- hammer

- 1½ in. (35-mm) galvanized flat-headed nails

- several small pieces of driftwood

- 1¼ in. (30 mm) copper flat-headed nails

- medium-sized paintbrush

- latex paint, in 2 contrasting colors

- medium-grade sandpaper

- wood wax

- metal-cutters or tin-snips

- piece of zinc roofing

- a length of ⅛-in. (2-mm) galvanized wire, for hanging the house

Encourage birds to visit your garden with this delightful birdhouse, which requires only basic carpentry skills. Alternatively, you can buy an unfinished birdhouse and paint it in your own color scheme, then add details such as a chimney, weathervane, and flags.

Most of the materials are reclaimed from dumpsters and beachcombing expeditions, and for the paint you can use some left over from larger projects. No two birdhouses will be the same, and two or three hung on a tree (or from an outside wall out of the reach of cats) will make colorful focal points in a garden.

1 Using a pencil, mark two identical "houseshapes" (an equilateral triangle on top of a square) on the floorboard. Use a triangle to check the 45° angles. Cut out with a saw, then cut another piece for the base. Using a drill with a hole-cutter attachment, cut a large hole in the center front for the entrance and a small hole the diameter of the doweling immediately below it. The size of the entrance hole depends on the birds you wish to attract.

Left: Extra perches can be glued or nailed onto the bird-house. Here, a tiny piece of sheet copper has been cut to make a fluttering pennant.

2 Nail the base to the front and back of the box, using galvanized nails. Saw pieces of driftwood for the sides of the box and attach with copper nails. Insert the doweling in the small hole to form a perch.

3 Paint the outside of the box with latex paint and leave to dry, then paint a contrasting coat of latex paint on top. When completely dry, rub down the surface with sandpaper until the paint color underneath begins to show through and the heads of the copper nails are visible. Paint around the entrance again with the first color so that the birds will see it. Apply a generous coat of wax over all the exterior surfaces.

VARIATION

Adapt the basic shape to make different sizes and styles, based on vernacular architecture and fantasy houses from imagination or memory.

4 Using metal-cutters or tin-snips, cut the zinc roofing to give a good overlap on all sides of the box. Place the zinc over the box and crease it along the center to match the top. Mark the middle of the crease and also two places where the zinc roof will meet the sides of the box. Remove the zinc and punch holes with a nail through the marks. Knot one end of the wire and thread it up through the center hole, for hanging the birdhouse. Finally, replace the zinc roof on the box, lining up the holes at the sides, and attach it with copper nails.

RUSTIC MIRROR

Mirrors multiply light, giving it an energy that will bring a dark corner of the garden to life. Even a small mirror can be positioned to accentuate another feature or the texture of the bark on a tree, but do not make the mirror too large or place it where birds may be disoriented and fly into it.

Reclaimed wood, such as old floor joists, has a robust, chunky character which is ideal for outdoors. Do not worry about small gaps where the boards join as they contribute to the effect and will be disguised by paint. If the wood you are using has not already been treated, apply a coat of preservative before assembling the frame.

You can decorate the finished mirror with shells, small stones, tiny mosaic tiles, or glass beads threaded onto galvanized or copper wire.

Right: Hung in the center of a wooden trellis panel, the mirror blends with its surroundings and reflects a tiny section of the garden beyond.

73

MATERIALS AND EQUIPMENT

- 2 x 10 in. (25 cm) lengths and 2 x 2 ft. (60 cm) lengths of reclaimed wood, approximately 2 in. (5 cm) thick and 4 in. (10 cm) wide

- right-angled triangle

- waterproof wood glue

- hammer

- 3-in. (75-mm) common nails

- medium-sized paintbrush

- white acrylic primer

- fine-grade sandpaper

- wood wax

- safety goggles

- router with rabbeting bit

- 7 x 20 in. (18 x 51 cm) piece of mirror glass

- glazing sprigs (small, specialized nails to hold the mirror in place)

- 1¼-in. (30-mm) galvanized screws

- a length of 1¼-in. (30-mm) galvanized wire, for hanging the mirror

1 Place one long and one short piece of wood together at right angles, checking the angle with the triangle. Smear a little glue along the inside edges where the two meet, then lay one piece on a level surface with the other piece vertically on top, edge to edge. Hammer in two nails on either side at an angle, so that they secure the wood underneath. Repeat with the other two pieces to make a box frame.

2 Paint the frame with acrylic primer and leave to dry. Rub with sandpaper until the grain of the wood begins to show through. Apply a generous layer of wax to give an effective waterproof coating.

VARIATION

Here two shades of green latex paint have been sponged onto the frame, exactly matching the colors of the variegated ivy surrounding it. The candle is held in place using the coiled wire holder on pages 84–86.

3 Wearing safety goggles and using a router with a rabbeting bit, make a rabbet on the back of the frame in which the mirror glass will sit comfortably. Alternatively, take the frame to a woodworker and ask them to cut a rabbet.

4 Carefully slide the mirror glass into place and secure firmly with glazing sprigs and plenty of glue around all the edges. Insert a screw on either side of the top back of the frame and link a piece of wire between the two for hanging the mirror.

lighting

There are numerous ways to make an outside space take on a magical appearance at night. Choose from the simple glow of a votive candle to the romantic twinkle of trees swathed in Christmas-tree lights. For a sophisticated approach, you could plan an electrical scheme integrated into walls and/or flooring. Judicious use of artificial light can silhouette trees and plants, dramatize a water feature, or create an intimate dining space.

LEFT   The most evocative and romantic form of outdoor lighting is also the most ancient. Candlelight is warm, flattering to faces, and has a hypnotic quality that induces calm and relaxation.

Above: Nothing artificial can compare to the beauty of natural light and the way it brings static objects to life, giving them a gentle and beguiling luminosity.

The light an outdoor space receives depends on the aspect—the direction in which the site faces. The amount of sunlight will vary depending on the latitude and the time of year, and the amount of shade will be affected by overhanging trees, high walls, and nearby buildings. Understanding the effects of light and shade should be an important part of your design for both people and plants.

A simple compass reading will allow you to determine where the sun rises and sets, and careful observation on a clear day will indicate the sunniest areas and which parts are subject to shade. Armed with this information, you can then designate the best places for seating and dining, as well as choosing which are the most appropriate plants to grow. Remember that the direction of the prevailing winds is also a factor, so even if there is plenty of sunlight, you may still need to provide shelter for people and delicate plants.

After the sun has set, artificial lighting is a dramatic way of extending the potential of your outside space, whether it be a small terrace or a large garden that is full of trees and shrubs. The problem with artificial outdoor lighting, however, is that the overall effect all too often looks false and even garish. It is therefore important to plan the lighting as carefully as the rest of the space and to incorporate different kinds of light in your design. The two most common reasons for using outside illumination are security and aesthetics, and you may need to combine these seemingly disparate criteria in one lighting scheme.

Above: The shadows cast by bamboo leaves make a decorative pattern against a sunlit fence. This is constructed from bamboo canes and held in place by poles.

In the winter the outside space is viewed mainly from the inside and can be lit accordingly. At the height of summer, many people enjoy gardening in the evening, which may be the only time when the temperature is cool enough for tasks such as weeding. There is also something very relaxing and soothing about watering a garden by the light of the moon, either real or artfully created.

Following the sun

In perfect conditions, it makes sense to link the outside space and the interior of the house by means of a terrace, creating a seamless transition between the two. However, in many situations, and particularly in an urban location, the sunniest and least shaded area may in fact be the one farthest away from the house.

Besides being the obvious location for relaxing and entertaining, a sunny patch at the end of the garden can also become the site for a more permanent structure. Set apart from the house, an outside room has all the attraction of a complete retreat, provided it is adequately equipped with power sources and linked to the home with some form of hard surface.

Before laying a path, consider the types of power equipment you need, such as conduits for lighting cables and for an exterior electrical outlet. If you plan ahead in this way, an outdoor room can be as user-friendly as any indoor room, with the means to plug into music, make coffee, and toast a sandwich.

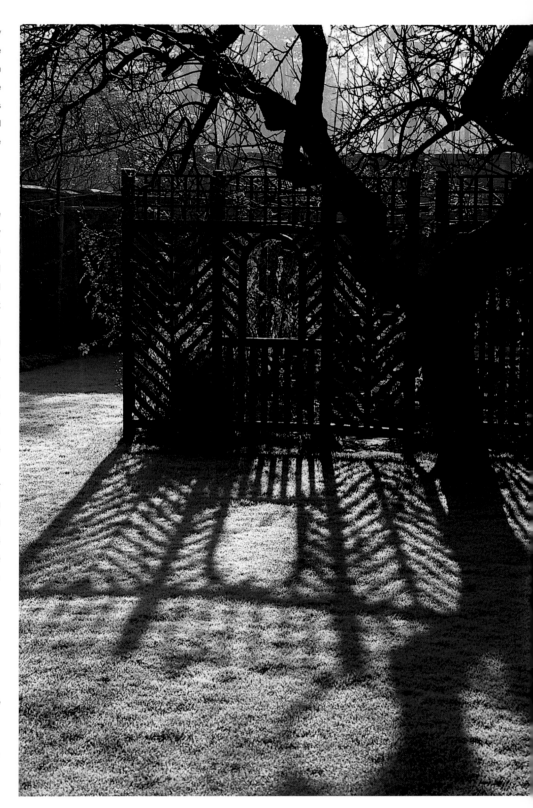

Right: The basic framework of a garden is most apparent In the winter months. The frosted white lawn shown here emphasizes the shadow patterns of the bare-branched trees and the herringbone design of the trellis.

Candlelight

When the weather is warm, outdoor living and entertaining can be extended long after sunset. Pressing a switch for instant electric light is convenient, but the most attractive source of artificial light, both inside and out, is undoubtedly candles. Their gently flickering glow is romantic and flattering to both faces and food, and it is the cheapest and easiest form of lighting to use.

For a very small financial outlay, you can put scores of votives in jam jars or small glass tumblers. Suspend them on wires from branches or the horizontal bars of trellis, line them up in rows along the top of a wall, tuck them into the corners of step risers, or make a continuous snake along the contours of a path. Metal storm lanterns are also excellent outdoors because, as with glass jars, the flame is protected. Many designs are available, from the highly decorative shapes made in India and Mexico to the more utilitarian styles found at camping equipment stores.

A patio or terrace with a solid or beamed roof will provide a support for a candle-lit chandelier, but it needs to be completely protected from any wind if the candles are to stay alight. If the evening is completely still, push a generous group of candles or patio torches into a terra cotta pot or galvanized bucket filled with sand. Patio torches are designed to withstand a reasonable amount of wind and will burn for several hours. Always be careful with outdoor candles and torches in case a gust of wind causes a spurt of hot wax, or burns plants or furniture. Naked flames must never be left unattended and should be extinguished with a candlesnuffer.

Many patio torches are impregnated with citronella oil, which discourages the mosquitoes and gnats that are attracted by candles on summer evenings. The distinctive smell does not appeal to everyone, so instead you can vaporize lemongrass essential oil in an oil burner. Another alternative is eucalyptus, which is planted in swampy areas in North Africa to deter mosquitoes from breeding.

The marriage of candlelight and water is a simple, inexpensive, and very effective way to create some atmospheric lighting. The still surface of a small pond, for example, will come alive at night if you decorate it with an enchanting flotilla of floating candles. Or on a smaller scale, you could create a table centerpiece with a shallow bowl of water containing scented floating candles. For a touch of romance, add some fragrant rose heads pinned onto tiny corks to make them float. An additional benefit of combining candles with water is that the flames will be safely extinguished when the candles burn down.

Above (top): These accordion-style Japanese paper lanterns offer practical protection from the wind.

Above (bottom): This more contemporary alternative uses fireproofed paper bags which are half filled with sand to make a firm base for a votive.

Left: During the day, cool air flows freely through the triangular recesses of a wall section resembling a fretwork window screen. These tiny shelves then serve as individual niches for glass lanterns to illuminate the terrace by night. The perfume wafting from a bowl of floating candles is enhanced with the fresh scent of rose petals.

Security lighting

This kind of lighting is primarily for deterring intruders. It is usually activated by movement and is linked to an alarm, which is clearly audible from inside the house. To be effective, it needs to highlight vulnerable areas such as the perimeter of the area and the exits and entrances.

It is advisable to have a separate system for security lighting, which can be activated when the property is unoccupied and is operated by a master switch in a convenient place inside the house.

Creating a mood

Atmospheric lighting needs to be more subtle. You can make an outside space look as though it is lit naturally by the moon and stars, or you can sensitively accent light it with uplights and spotlights.
If a garden has a large, mature tree, this offers the potential to create a nighttime canopy of tiny lights resembling twinkling stars. Alternatively, larger downlights can be used to make shadow patterns on the ground. The electric cables that feed these lights are best wound around and attached to the tree trunk with plastic plant ties, fixed with stainless steel nails. The plant ties will allow the cables room for movement as the trunk grows and expands. Where the cable meets the ground, it should be buried in a protective conduit and run back to its source along a route where it is unlikely to be disturbed by cultivation. Remember that the positioning of the light fixtures must be accessible, so that you can replace bulbs, but that long-life outdoor bulbs (lasting about 24,000 hours) will make maintenance much easier.

The most unobtrusive method of lighting the ground where you are likely to walk is by using recessed uplights. Such light fittings emit a glow that is bright enough to make the surrounding ground clearly visible without creating a blinding upward shaft of light. An inexpensive method of concealing uplights is to place them in small terra cotta pots so that the cable runs through the drainage holes.

Some garden lights are adjustable and are fitted to a rigid plastic spike so that they can be angled to highlight shrubs or ornaments. It is a great advantage to be able to highlight different parts of your outdoor space at different times of the year. One effective mobile system is provided by solar-powered garden lights, which require no wiring; instead, the sunlight charges a battery via a solar panel, which in turn lights the lamp after dark.

Above: This is a contemporary lighting scheme with uplights and recessed downlights which are virtually invisible. The subtle effect integrates the glass-fronted house with the exterior.

Left: Functional lighting can also be used to give a decorative quality to an outside area. This row of glare-free lights illuminates the flight of brick steps.

Below: A vertical structure such as this can be constructed and used to provide a conduit through which a power circuit can be concealed.

The technicalities

Artificial lighting is a science—but not one to be intimidated by. Installation is best left to a professional electrician, but the effects also need to be designed to suit the style of the garden or terrace.

Low-voltage circuits are ideal for small outside spaces where only short cable runs are required. The system is fitted with a transformer, which lowers the voltage, making the supply safer. Low-voltage lights tend to be small and, if strategically placed, are barely visible during the day.

However well you have planned your lighting, it is wise to keep a record of all the power circuits in the space. This will be particularly useful for future owners. The best route for power circuits is to follow the perimeter of a terrace or the edges of paths, which is the logical place to install lighting.

Because of their location, outdoor lights must be completely weatherproof. Many bathroom fixtures and the heavy-duty lights found at marine-supply stores are also practical in an outdoor space.

RECYCLED GLASS LANTERNS

Candlelight is especially evocative in a garden space, where the flickering flames create a magical atmosphere and give instant light. Hang a row of these lovely lanterns from metal hooks across a terrace or from the branches of a tree. However, take care to space them out, to prevent a gust of wind from causing them to clash together and shatter.

Apart from a bottle-cutter, the only materials needed are empty glass bottles and wire. White-wine and mineral-water bottles work best, as the candlelight is visible through the clear glass. The lanterns become very hot when the candles are alight, so wait until they have burned out before attempting to remove the glass, or use oven gloves. Never leave burning candles unattended, even in the garden.

VARIATION

Without the wire and with the addition of a metal brioche pan, the bottle makes a hurricane lamp for a tiny candle. Make sure the surface you stand it on is heat-resistant.

MATERIALS AND EQUIPMENT

- clear or pale-colored round glass bottles, with clearly defined necks

- bottle-cutter

- coarse emery paper or a small silicon-carbide stone (as used to sharpen knives)

- wire-cutters

- a length ⅛-in.(2-mm) galvanized wire

- small tin can, approximately 2 in.(5 cm) diameter

- votive candles

- pliers

1 Wash and dry the bottles, removing any labels. Adjust the height of the bottle-cutter to where you wish to cut the bottle. Tighten all the screws, then revolve the blade and make one continuous score line. Experiment on spare bottles, if necessary, until you perfect the technique.

2 Insert the "tapper" and line up the small washer inside the bottle exactly opposite the score line. Press the disk down into the neck of the bottle, and start tapping very gently. Continue tapping until the two parts of the bottle separate.

3 The cut end of the bottle is razor-sharp, so rub it down carefully with emery paper. Alternatively, use a small silicon-carbide stone to smooth the rim.

4 Cut a piece of wire approximately twice the length of the bottle, and straighten it as much as possible. Push it up inside the bottle, then make a double kink to hold the wire in place inside the neck.

5 Twist the lower end of the wire around a small can to make symmetrical coils, somewhat like a metal bedspring. This will be the candle-holder for the votive.

6 Adjust the lower coils by winding them more tightly until the votive fits snugly and is perfectly level. Insert the wire and votive into the bottle. Using pliers, twist the top of the wire to make a hook for hanging.

Left: Even in a breeze, the lantern stays alight, and the flickering flames cast attractive reflections through the glass.

SCENTED CHANDELIER

Fill a hanging basket with tiny Christmas-tree lights and sweet-scented plants to softly illuminate and perfume a sunroom or terrace. Glass droplets tied with invisible fishing line sparkle in the lights and chime like the sound of chinking glasses.

Ideally, plant up the basket when the plants are in full bud, so that the flowers will open in situ. Once they have faded, the jasmine can be planted outside in warm zones; the stephanotis, which originates in Madagascar, will need a minimum temperature of 59° F (15° C).

MATERIALS AND EQUIPMENT

- lights, with transformer
- metal hanging basket
- bucket
- thin fuse wire or florist's wire
- moss
- scissors
- basket liner
- 2 *Stephanotis floribunda* plants
- 3 *Jasminum polyanthum* plants
- transparent fishing line
- glass droplets

1 Low-voltage outdoor lights must be plugged only into an outlet that is indoors and protected by an approved circuit-breaker. Unwind the lights and make sure that they are working. (Turn the lights off at the main when replacing faulty bulbs.) Place the hanging basket in a bucket to keep it steady, then wire the lights to the sides and base of the basket. Take care to keep the bulbs separate from each other.

2 Line the basket with a layer of moss, and push firmly into the sides. Cut a circle of liner that will slightly overlap the top of the basket.

3 The single stem of a stephanotis plant is often trained over a wire frame. Remove this carefully, and re-plant in the basket. Wind the stem around the perimeter of the basket, holding it securely with wire but without tying it so tightly that it damages the stem. Add the other stephanotis and the jasmine plants.

Left: As the daylight fades, the lights in the chandelier will start to become visible, and the power of the flowers' perfume will also increase.

4 Switch on the lights and make sure that they are not touching. Then switch the lights off and hang the basket in place. Switch them on again, and thread a length of fishing line onto each glass droplet and suspend them at differing levels from the sides and bottom of the basket.

89

water

We have a deep affinity with water. It both stimulates and relaxes our senses and can be a vital element in the contemporary outside room. There is something intrinsically soothing about the sight of reflections on an expanse of still water; the sound of a softly gurgling fountain, bubbling up among smooth stones; or the sensation of sitting in a hot tub under the stars. Water can create excitement with sound and stimulation, or it can be used to induce a cool atmosphere of calming relaxation.

LEFT As this sheet of water cascades from a simple spout, it recreates the sound of a waterfall and radiates sprays of tiny droplets caught sparkling in the sunlight.

Water is a great and universal source of attraction. The ancient gardens of the Islamic world symbolized paradise on earth, as instructed in the writings of the Koran, and featured the same rhythmic geometrical patterns found on oriental carpets. Those gardens represented an escape from the harshness of the desert, so water was an essential element, cooling the air and creating much-needed humidity. Fine examples of traditional Islamic water and shade gardens can still be seen at the Alhambra in Granada, Spain, and at the Palace of Almudaina in Palma, Majorca. Although created more than 500 years ago, their engineering and their classic lines and perfect proportions continue to influence landscape design today.

The pleasure we derive from taking a bath or shower, and experiencing the sight and smell of the sea, confirms the close affinity we feel with water. It stimulates and relaxes all our senses, restoring our sense of well-being. Contemporary bathroom design has moved on from its functional roots to embrace a more eastern influence, in which time is taken to enjoy the simple pleasures of bathing.

This fascination with water extends outdoors, where designers, architects, and sculptors are using modern technology and materials to create fantastic effects. A contemporary water feature has now risen to the top of the list of popular focal points and ornaments for the garden.

Right: Designed with careful precision and related to the proportions of the architecture, a swimming pool is both a luxurious outdoor bathroom and a still blue surface, reflecting the ever-changing sky.

Left: A sybaritic delight. The perfect inside and outside bathroom, where you can bathe in the internal shade or shower in the fresh air and sunshine.

Below: A non-slip border between the edge of the swimming pool and the raised deck provides a well-considered safety element.

Outdoor pools and tubs

Depending on the space available, the benefits of water can be enjoyed outside in a heated swimming pool, a hot tub fitted with powerful jets for muscle-soothing hydrotherapy, or a simple outdoor shower for refreshing drenches.

The construction of a swimming pool is best left to professionals, and careful consideration needs to be given to its design, its relationship to sur-rounding buildings, and safety provisions. In hot climates where a pool is the center of an outside lifestyle virtually all year round, it makes sense to site it near the house. Even in cooler climes, if the pool is sufficiently heated it can be used when there is snow on the ground, provided there is only a short dash to a warm area. Whatever the size of the pool, it must be regarded as a high-maintenance feature with continuous running costs for the filtra-tion and skimmer systems, plus additional expenses if the water is to be kept permanently heated.

Smaller projects such as a hot tub require little space. A tub could be integrated into the design for a small, secluded courtyard or positioned on a roof terrace that is not overlooked—privacy is obviously an important requirement for outdoor bathing. Inspi-

ration for the design of a hot tub can be found in traditional Japanese bathrooms, which often feature natural materials such as stone and wood which are appropriate in an exterior setting.

Above: A natural pond and wildlife paradise is all but concealed by the dense cover of moisture-loving plants, particularly alchemilla mollis, *which cascades over the stone edges, providing a place for birds and animals to drink.*

Ponds

A graveled garden is ideal for installing the simplest of all water features, a shallow pond, with the minimum of disruption. Traditional Japanese gardens often combine a water feature with gravel or slate chips, naturally smoothed in rivers. Slate's dark color contrasts well with surrounding green plants. A great advantage of a loose-stoned or a grassed garden is that any electric cables required for lighting, or a pump, can be conveniently and inexpensively concealed underneath. Ideally, conduits to carry power cables should be included in the initial plans for an outside space. It would be inconceivable to build a house without making provision for plumbing and electricity, yet these vital elements are often overlooked when planning a garden. If you are laying a paved area, it costs very little to include a length of plastic conduit beneath the paving through which power cables can be fed if necessary at a later stage.

Designing an outside space to include a water feature will have a dramatic effect on the style of planting. It will open up the possibilities of using moisture-loving and marginal plants, as well as those that require total submersion of their roots and those that float on the surface of the water.

High-quality, long-life PVC (polyvinyl chloride) fabrics and butyl (isobutylene isoprene rubber) liners have made the construction of informal pools a simple do-it-yourself project that can be completed in a few hours. Bought by the yard, these liners are guaranteed to last for at least 20 years, and being (usually) black, they give excellent surface reflections. Using a liner, you can design a formal pond with straight edges and vertical sides topped with stone slabs or sympathetic paving. These need to overhang the water enough to conceal the liner beneath. Alternatively, you can create a more free-form shape with stepped shelves around the perimeter for marginal and bog plants, or a sloping "pebble beach" edge where birds and animals can drink and bathe.

If toddlers and young children play in the garden, great care must be taken to ensure that any water feature is perfectly safe. A small pond can be filled with large stones to just below the waterline

Left: Water is a major feature in the Japanese garden. The ponds are often relatively shallow and are described by the term kage ike, or "mirror pond." This is due to the underside curvature of a bridge being reflected in the still water below.

until the children are older. A deep pond can be covered with a removable fine metal mesh which, if positioned just below the water surface, is not too obtrusive. Such safety guards may also be necessary if you keep fish and there is a danger they may poached by herons.

Installing a fountain in a small reservoir is an attractive way to avoid the potential dangers of open water. A submersible pump sits at the bottom of a lined hole or pond and draws water in through an integral filter, pumping it out in a range of different spray patterns which can be adjusted to imitate the subtle gurgle of a natural spring. Standing the pump on a brick ensures that it is kept on a flat surface and prevents any dirt or sludge from the bottom of the pond from interfering with the pump mechanism. Most pumps are designed to run off the main electricity supply, and their cables, which are best laid underground, need to be protected inside a sturdy conduit, usually a rigid plastic pipe. The installation is best carried out by a qualified electrician, who will also install a circuit-breaker if you do not already have one.

The only drawback of a sunken pond is if the site has a naturally high water-table. After winter rainfall the level of underground water may raise the liner, causing it to balloon up out of the pond. In this case, it may be wiser to construct a raised pond or series of wide channels connected by concrete or decking wood walkways. Wooden decking has a natural affinity with water and creates a nautical style reminiscent of narrow piers and jetties in coastal harbors. If you construct the decking so that it overhangs the water, it will make the pond appear larger and give it a crisp contemporary shape.

A raised pond can also incorporate a wide edge broad enough for seating. If the site is sloping or uneven, a series of wooden decks would make an attractive link between a series of sunken and raised pools, in which the water is pumped and recycled from the lowest pond to the top. Ambitious projects like these are best carried out using professional help and advice.

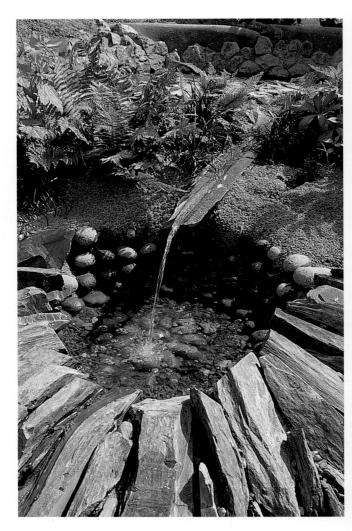

A precious resource

Water is too valuable a resource to waste, so every gardener needs to consider how best to utilize and conserve it. Most garden plants can in fact survive short spells of drought because their roots stretch deep down into the ground, and with a suitable mulch, very little of the water in the soil is lost through evaporation. But containers, especially those with a porous surface such as terra cotta, require watering as much as twice a day in summer. It would be foolhardy to plan a garden without an outside water source, especially if it is on a roof, where the drying effects of the wind can be as harmful as hot sun.

Above: Nature can be a wonderful source of inspiration for the design of contemporary water features. The bank of rounded pebbles contrasts with the radiating frame of slate.

Watering a small container garden by hand can be soothing, but it is also sensible to have a backup so that you are not obliged to stay at home all summer. Modern irrigation systems are designed to water specific areas and types of planting and can be linked to a feed option providing exact amounts of fertilizer. Many of the more sophisticated systems have environmental sensory devices that can detect when there has been sufficient rainfall or if there is a risk of freezing. Even a basic irrigation system, in which water is delivered to individual pots by means of a web of surface pipes attached to tiny sprays, can be connected to a 24-hour timer.

Left: In a tiny enclosed courtyard, the flowing water keeps good "chi" (energy) moving and reflects against the metallic plinth. The brimming pool creates a pleasant and cooling atmosphere.

Above: Underwater lighting can illuminate the bottom of a pool and reveal a mysterious world hidden below the surface, creating a wonderful environment for nocturnal swimming.

97

CONTAINER POND

This is an ideal water feature for a raised deck or roof terrace, where a permanent water feature would be impractical. Choose a container that suits the style and size of your space—a cool gray steel container looks very modern, but you could equally well use a shallow stone bowl or glazed ceramic jar. The silvery color of the container used here makes a bold contrast to a planting scheme of various shades and textures of foliage.

The plants are individually planted, so it is easy to rearrange or replace them. This scheme is designed for a warm environment, but in colder climates tender specimens can be wintered indoors or treated as annuals and bought fresh each year.

MATERIALS AND EQUIPMENT

- selection of marginal and aquatic plants

- plastic pots to suit the size of the plants

- sterile clay-based loam or aquatic potting mixture, well sieved

- aquatic gravel

- plastic bags

- stainless steel container

- rubber gloves

- clean bricks

- underwater light (optional)

PLANTS

- Cord grass (*Spartina pectinata* "Aureo marginata"), a hardy marginal plant that should be positioned with the top of the pot just below water level.

- Water lettuce (*Pistia stratiotes*) is a tender aquatic plant which will float at surface level in water 4–18 in. (10–45 cm) deep.

- Scouring rush or mare's horsetail (*Equisetum hyemale*) should be planted in 6 in. (15 cm) of water.

- Umbrella palm (*Cyperus alternifolius*) is a tender marginal plant which should be planted at water level. It may be treated as a houseplant in winter in a warm, steamy bathroom or kept well watered in a frost-free greenhouse.

- Chinese water chestnut (*Eleocharis dulcis* "Variegate") is a tender marginal plant which resembles a variegated rush and requires a planting depth of 6 in. (15 cm).

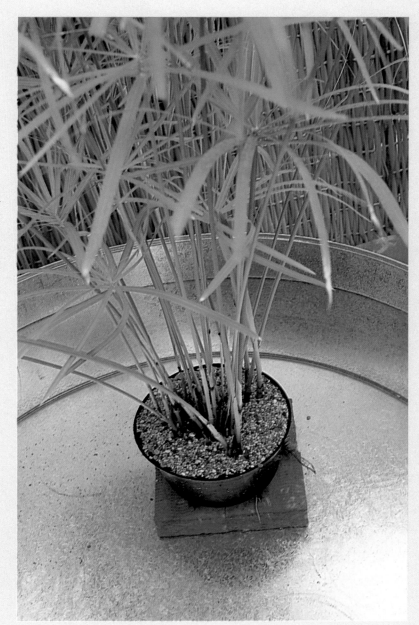

1 Place each of the marginal plants in a plastic pot large enough to allow plenty of room for growth. Fill each one with loam or potting mixture, leaving about 1¼ in. (3 cm) at the top for a mulch of aquatic gravel. The roots of aquatic plants get tangled together very easily, so keep each one in a plastic bag before planting. This also prevents damage through drying out.

2 Arrange the pots on dry land to make a pleasing composition. Fill the container with fresh water. Wearing rubber gloves, position the tallest plant, using bricks to achieve the optimum depth.

3 Add the rest of the pots, then fill in the gaps with floating aquatic plants.

4 Tall reeds, bamboos, and rushes planted in pots need shelter from wind because their roots will not give the same stability as if they were planted directly into the soil. They all thrive in good light but need protection from continuous hot sun, which will overheat the water.

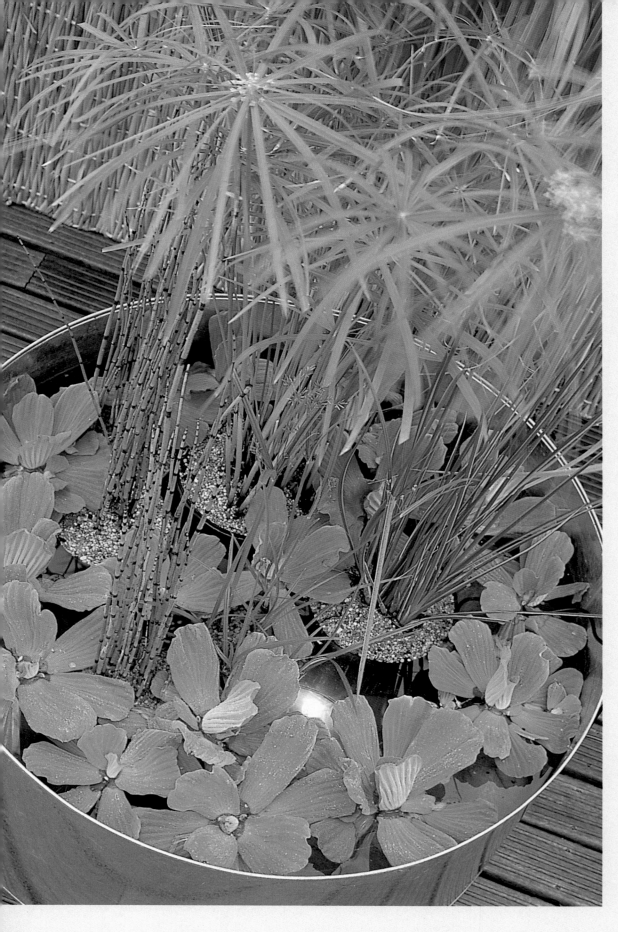

VARIATION

For a dramatic effect at night, place an underwater light at the bottom of the container. A low-voltage halogen light is the safest and very effective. It must be connected to an outlet indoors and protected by an approved circuit-breaker.

BUBBLE FOUNTAIN

Moving water and crushed glass are used to create a sparkling feature suitable for a limited space. The fountain springs up from a hole in the ground and trickles over large slate chips, surrounded by "ripples" of crushed glass and rings of smaller stones.

A small submersible pump will give spray heights of 12–36 in. (30–90 cm), the highest of which requires a pond diameter of only 36 in. (90 cm). The electrically powered pump is neat, quiet, and easy to install; it should be connected to an indoor outlet and protected by a circuit breaker. The fountain is relatively maintenance-free, but the reservoir must never be allowed to run dry, or the pump will burn out. The pump should not be operated or left outside in freezing conditions.

This water feature is not suitable in a garden with young children.

MATERIALS AND TOOLS

- 45 lb. (20 kg) fine sand
- butyl lining
- clean new brick
- submersible pump, with cable
- rigid wire mesh (as used for animal and bird cages)
- wire-cutters
- conduit for the pump cable and circuit-breaker
- 130 lb. (60 kg) of slate chips or similar material
- 88 lb. (40 kg) of ½-in. (1-cm) clear crushed glass
- 132 lb. (60 kg) of ½-in (1-cm) green crushed glass

Left: Commercially produced crushed glass, originally developed for aquariums, is wonderful when used as a garden mulch and within water features. It is quite safe for both plants and fish and is available in different colors and sizes.

1 Choose a site away from falling leaves. Dig a hole deep enough to submerge the entire pump when it is standing on the brick. Excavate the sides to a diameter of 3–4 ft. (90–120 cm), with a fall toward the central reservoir. Discard any loose stones and, unless the topsoil is very fine, cover the area with a layer of sand.

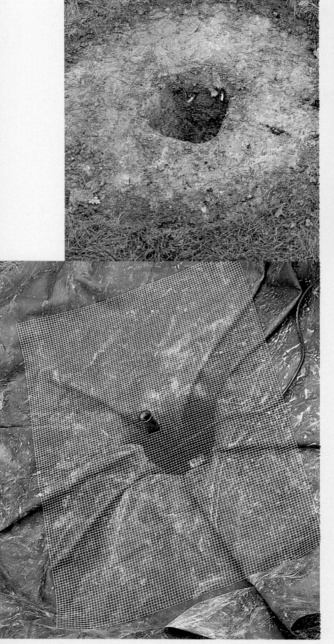

2 Place the lining in the hole, flattening it at the bottom, then pleat it in flat folds as it extends out of the hole. Leave the excess hanging over the edge. Place the brick in the hole with the pump on top. Make sure it is steady and level. Center the wire mesh over the hole, and using wire-cutters, cut out a small circle large enough for the pump stem to protrude through. Lay the cable generously over the lining until it reaches the edge, then feed it through the conduit, ideally buried out of sight, to the electrical source.

Right: The huge leaves of the giant prickly rhubarb (Gunnera manicata) growing behind the bubble fountain give a sense of mystery. These water-loving plants grow well in rich, moist bog garden soil.

3 Flood the excavated area with water, making sure that the reservoir is completely full. Test the pump and adjust the flow if necessary. While the pump is running, arrange the largest slate chips in a natural-looking ring. Make a thick mound of clear crushed glass around the stones, so that half are submerged and half are above the surface but glistening with spray. Add a ring of smaller stones, then a sloping mound of green crushed glass shaped like a gentle ripple. Conceal the edge with a ring of small slate chips. Trim the lining so that it is concealed under the slate.

decorating with plants

In many traditional gardens it is the plants, trees, and shrubs that create the design and atmosphere, but some outside spaces can employ plants to emphasize a decorative style or perform a specific function. A single tree, such as a tropical palm, can create a focal point; a raised bed filled with culinary herbs will provide constant fresh flavorings; and an evergreen climber can be used as a contrasting color to enhance the tone and texture of a wall or trellis.

LEFT   The perfectly symmetrical architectural form of the agave plant gives a strongly sculptural element to frost-free spaces.

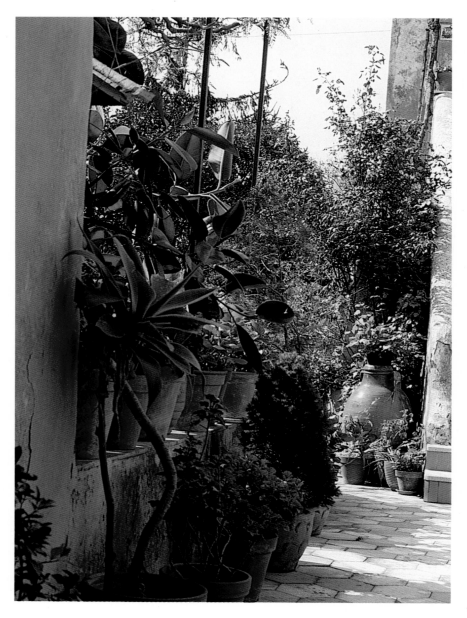

Successful gardening also depends on accurately analyzing the site so that you can choose plants that will be happy growing there. You can improve the soil and control the watering, but it is impossible to completely change the local climate. For a plant to be strong and healthy, it needs to be grown in a place that is as close as possible to its natural habitat.

Some of the most successful contemporary gardens contain only three or four different types of plant, complementing the simplicity of modern interiors. Having a clear idea of the style of outdoor space you wish to create will help you to formulate a shortlist of "must-have" plants. By a careful process of elimination, you can then narrow down the choice to find the right plant for any given position.

The right plant in the right place

A plant's natural environment is the main clue to its ideal planting position. Plants that would normally grow under trees are likely to thrive in a garden shaded by high walls and surrounding buildings, while plants that flourish in hot, windy coastal areas stand the best chance of tolerating the arid conditions found on exposed urban roof terraces. Even in the smallest space there will probably be some variation of light and shade, to which different plants will be suited.

If you want to grow a climber over an outside wall, a south- or west-facing wall is far preferable to one facing north or east, which will inevitably be colder and receive significantly less sun. Some climbers require no support, but others will need a trellis or an invisible framework of wires to scramble up. A wall will also be improved by a range of shrubs and trees that can be trained and pruned against it; tall, narrow shapes look particularly elegant. Shrubs with sharp thorns and impenetrable foliage provide security against intruders, and others offer summer scent and flowers at a time of the year when you are most likely to be outside.

Above: This sunbaked courtyard is an outside space that relies entirely on container-grown plants to create borders of lush, aromatic, and drought-tolerant plants. They are planted in similar terra cotta pots.

In outdoor spaces that are designed primarily for people, plants may need to fulfill a specific role as well as being decorative. Before you select each plant, it is a useful discipline to determine its contribution to your outside space as well as considering its appearance. Containers are invaluable, particularly in a small space, because they enable you to move shapes, colors, and textures around to create different effects.

Dedicated cooks may want to devote their available space to edible plants which, with careful planning, will provide home-grown produce for most of the year. Growing your own herbs is particularly satisfying and economical, as most of them require very little space, and frequent picking stimulates more generous growth. Mixing ornamental flowers with lettuces and vegetables is an attractive way to combine the practical with the decorative, and certain kinds of companion planting will deter destructive insects and encourage pollinating bees.

Left: The perimeter is the strongest part of this roof terrace. Specially-made lightweight containers soften the hard edges of the safety barrier and also provide a degree of privacy.

Above: Edible plants like kale, chard, and the riotous nasturtiums can be intermingled with more decorative plants, particularly those that deter unwanted destructive insects.

Designing with color

Flowers and leaves have inspiring scents and shapes, but the initial impact from a garden or outdoor space is usually one of color. Most flowers and deciduous shrubs and trees are short-lived, temporarily changing the permanent color scheme of walls, floor surfaces, outdoor furniture, and evergreens. Even evergreen is not one color, but a whole range of shades and tones to add to your palette. A successful exterior color scheme is thus a subtle relationship between nature and the fabricated elements. The architecture of an adjoining building and the tone and texture of the exterior woodwork and masonry are essential ingredients in an outside color scheme. Some of these elements are fixed, but by painting a wall or trellis, or adding a different floor covering or style of furniture, you can add a permanent color that will enhance all the colors around it.

Below: The red buds and pink flowers of primula vialii *are short-lived, but they still make a spectacular display for a few weeks in summer. An ideal candidate for a large container.*

As for the flowers and foliage, it is a misguided notion that all plant combinations are pleasing. In the wild, flowers and plants tend to create their own natural harmony, but many of the modified colors of cultivated hybrids are not what nature intended. Exotic imported plants look attractive in a garden center, but they do not always integrate happily into every climate. If in doubt, remember that plants that naturally grow together are more likely to create a pleasing effect.

The quality and quantity of natural light has a dramatic effect on how we perceive colors. An outside space that makes the most of the changing light throughout the day will give added dimension to the colors within it. Hot, flame colors zing out in the midday sun but are lost in the evening shadows, when blues and purples radiate a subtle luminescence, as do all shades of white, silver, and cream. Strong, bright colors are perfect against the brilliant blue sky in countries such as Greece, where dazzling white-washed walls, acid lime-green painted wood, and vibrant pink bougainvilleas are an exciting combination, but they lose their impact in the softer, slanting light of northern Europe, which is more sympathetic to subtle pastel tones. Daylight varies enormously, depending on the time of day and the season, and the amount of shade also determines the effect of different colors.

Left: Plants are visually more effective when placed and repeated in large blocks. Their flowers and foliage combined make a greater impact on the sight and their colors, textures, and hues, create a more harmonious effect.

Creating an instant effect

A new garden, traditionally planted, will take several years to reach maturity, but an outside room can include some judicious cheating to realize a finished result much sooner. Buying mature plants and trees is expensive, but worthwhile if you consider that you are paying for the years a nursery or specialist grower has taken to raise and tend them. Specialists may also be able to offer expert advice on the most suitable species for your space and location. A single ten-year-old tree would make an impressive focal point on a paved terrace, while a tall thicket of lush bamboo would create instant shade and shelter around a seating area.

Many trees and shrubs will thrive quite happily in containers, and you have the option of taking them with you if you move to another house. To do well in pots, plants need to be either slow-growing by nature or pruned to maintain a balance between the size of the roots and the amount of foliage. Hardy exotics such as palms and fatsia are slow-growing, whereas bay (*Laurus nobilis*), olive (*Olea europaea*), common box (*Buxus sempervirens*), and the strawberry tree (*Arbutus unedo*) can be clipped into distinctive shapes—balls, pyramids, mopheads, and lollipops. These topiary shapes restrict the plants' size at the same time as giving them a strong, attractive outline. Other plants, including the many varieties of grasses and bamboo, have such invasive root systems that they are better off contained in pots.

Containers have maximum flexibility in that they are reasonably easy to move. If you are at all uncertain about the designing of your gardening scheme, it is a great advantage to be able to look at individual plants in the context of

Left: The curvaceous contours of gigantic pots illustrate the importance of selecting containers for their aesthetic merit and not just as vessels to hold plants. Used singly or grouped together, they contribute to outside decoration and style.

other features in the outdoor space, and to be able to move them into different combinations. Containers allow such experimentation.

It is almost impossible to choose a container that is too big for a space; one huge pot will look far more impressive than scores of small ones. Another advantage of buying big is that, even left unplanted, a large amphora or curvaceous urn has the dramatic presence of an elegant sculpture. Place it at a central focal point, in a corner to soften hard vertical lines, or at the end of a path to create a vista. The space afforded by a large container allows you to grow masses of one plant for greater impact or to grow one tall permanent tree or shrub. If you opt for the latter, you can still provide seasonal interest by underplanting with bulbs and annuals. But remember that although "big," in the context of containers, can be beautiful, it will also be heavy.

The value of contained spaces

Container gardening is not only about growing plants in pots; it can also be perceived as planting in contained spaces such as a raised bed, a narrow strip between a wall and paving, crevices among stones and slabs, a water feature, or a graveled area. A great advantage of contained gardening is that the level of maintenance can be manipulated. In a contained area the soil quality can easily be improved, watering is more localized, and the type and density of planting can be controlled.

The height of a raised bed dramatically changes the scale and proportions of a small space. If you incorporate seating alongside the bed, the plants will feel closer and more intimate, an effect that is enhanced if you grow scented varieties. Raised areas lend themselves to strategic seasonal planting. For example, in early spring you could look out across a raised bed to view the whole of the space beyond, whereas later in the year you could create a living screen of tall plants to divide one part of the garden from another. Fast-growing annuals such as fennel (*Foeniculum vulgare*) and sunflowers (*Helianthus annus*) reach well over 6 ft. (2 m) in a couple of months, as do perennials such as *Verbena bonariensis* (perennial in warmer zones), and meadow rue (*Thalictrum rochebruneanum*), which should then be cut back in the winter. Raised beds also offer numerous advantages to the vegetable gardener. They are far less backbreaking to tend, and many of the pests that plague edibles at ground level, such as carrot fly, slugs, and snails, are easier to control organically on a contained, higher level.

If you have a narrow space between a wall and paving, this is an ideal position for a single-layer climber, which you can easily keep well trained. Mulch the ground at its feet with a thick layer of stones or gravel, using a color to blend with the color of the paving, and this will prevent water evaporation and suppress weeds. If you

deliberately leave sufficient space when laying paving stones on a terrace, small alpines or mat-forming plants will colonize very freely.

In a gravel garden, pots can be concealed in deep planting pockets covered by stones, which makes the plants easier to move or divide when they outgrow their individual containers. The

Above: Combining plants successfully takes as much skill as fusing food flavors or coordinating colors. A perfect union is the vibrant agapanthus and the skeletal eryngium.

same principle can be applied to water features, where plants considered to be invasive are held in check by being kept contained in pots, partially or completely submerged in the water. As with dry-land container gardening, plants can be grouped together and rearranged when one fades and another reaches its prime.

Roof Terraces

Weight is an important consideration on roof terraces and balconies. Ask a structural engineer or architect to calculate weight-loading capacity, which will depend on the number and size of beams in the roof or the balcony's structure. The edge of a roof is the strongest part, so the ideal planting solution is a container that runs around the perimeter. This will also create a solid safety barrier if the roof is enclosed by railings instead of a wall. The back of the container could serve as a fixing point for a screen of trellis, on which climbing plants would give shelter and privacy. If the roof has a timber deck, a wooden planter made from the same flooring material would fit in well. Wind is usually a problem on roof gardens, so unless the space is completely sheltered, it is vital to create a windbreak. Choose plants with tough foliage or those that are small and compact, and will not be ruffled by gusts and gales. Remember that however drought- and wind-resistant your choice of planting, it is untenable to consider rooftop gardening without an easily accessible source of water.

Whether at roof level or on the ground, contained and container plants cannot develop deep enough root systems to survive prolonged spells of drought. Contained gardening is therefore high maintenance, but there are likely to be considerably fewer plants than in a traditional garden, so it may be viable to install an automatic watering and feeding system. Watering by hand can also be very satisfying, and is usually only necessary when the weather encourages you to be in the fresh air enjoying your outside space.

Left: An Aegean-blue stained wood window box complements the subtle greens of flowering echeveria and blueish-gray Agave americana.

Below: On a rooftop, the tall galvanized containers complement the lead flashings. The gray Festuca glauca *resembles billowing smoke.*

DECORATED POTS

Most perennial herbs, particularly those Mediterranean natives that flourish in a well-drained light soil and a sheltered, sunny position, are ideal candidates for container gardening. Woody-stemmed herbs such as lavender can be trained as decorative topiary balls, and the silvery gray-green foliage is enhanced by painting clay flowerpots with a pale pistachio-colored latex paint with a broad white band to complement a white gravel mulch.

MATERIALS AND TOOLS

- 3 clay or pale terra cotta pots
- pale green latex flat paint
- white acrylic paint
- soil-based potting mixture
- 3 pot-grown lavender plants
- white pea gravel
- metal tray
- paintbrush
- masking tape

1 Brush off any loose material on the pots, and ensure the surface is dry. Paint the outside and top few inches inside the pot with a generous layer of pale green paint. Leave the pots to dry for at least 24 hours in a cool, well-aired place. Mask off an area under the rim approximately 1 in. (2.5 cm) wide. Paint the strip you have masked off with the white acrylic paint. Using short pieces of overlapping tape helps to keep the edges of the band straight and parallel.

2 Remove the pieces of tape very carefully when the paint is completely dry. Plant the lavender, leaving space at the top of each pot for a generous layer of pea-gravel mulch. Add a layer of gravel to the metal tray, and place the pots on top.

Above: Light, protective gloves should always be worn when applying gilding material.

VARIATIONS

A burnished effect around the rim can be created by using a gilding material with a wax base.

Seashells and smooth rounded beach pebbles make an alternative mulch.

Other suitable plants include topiarized rosemary bushes, which would also be useful for culinary purposes.

115

VARIATIONS

Above: A metal container can be customized using the same masking technique as the painted pots by using metallic or car spray paint.

Right: The color and shape of these *Bellis perennis* (English daisy) flowers is repeated on the painted terra cotta pot with the addition of a flat white shell, glued in place with waterproof adhesive.

TWO-TIER CONTAINER

If space is at a premium, it is vital to make the most of it, vertically and horizontally. For example, a large square or rectangular container will fit snugly into the corner of a balcony and provide more room for plants than a collection of small circular pots.

A two-tier container gives the opportunity for temporary planting in the top tier, which can be changed each season without disrupting the permanent display below. The top tier can be considered somewhat like a vase, in which plants are replaced after flowering. Scented plants such as lilies and nicotiana, whose perfume increases after dusk, are especially welcome in a small space. Another attractive idea is to grow perennial herbs in the bottom tier, with annual herbs such as chervil or basil in the top. You could also grow acid-loving plants in one tier, and plants that prefer alkaline conditions in the other.

Right: The oyster-shell mulch helps to retain the moist environment that fragrant lily-of-the-valley (Convallaria majalis) prefer.

Right: Glass panels set into the metal barrier protect flowers and foliage from the desiccating effect of wind, which is most plants' worst enemy.

MATERIALS AND EQUIPMENT

- 2 different-sized stainless steel or galvanized containers, in similar style

- metal punch

- coarse grit

- bricks (optional)

- good-quality sterile potting mixture

- selection of permanent plants, e.g. lacecap hydrangea (*Hydrangea macrophylla*) and variegated ivy (*Hedera helix*), and temporary plants, e.g. lily-of-the-valley (*Convallaria majalis*)

- oyster shells

1 Containers dry out in warm weather, but they can also become waterlogged, which will make the roots of the plants rot. Pierce several rows of small holes in the base of the large container. Spread a thick layer of coarse grit in the bottom to allow excess water to drain away.

2 It is easier to position the smaller top container before planting up the lower tier. Depending on the height of the plants in the top tier, you may want to raise the small container on a couple of bricks.

3 Fill both containers with potting mixture. Plant the hydrangea and ivy in the lower tier, then plant the lily-of-the-valley in the top. Cover the compost with a layer of oyster shells as a decorative mulch.

4 A two-tier container filled with plants and soil is very difficult to move without dismantling it. One solution is to place your container on a small mobile platform, preferably with braked castors. This is extremely useful when you want to move it in and out of the shade in hot weather.

5 In winter, the root balls of container-grown plants may need to be insulated. Line the inside of each container with pieces of thin polystyrene sheet, or wrap the outside with several layers of burlap tied in place with string. In severe weather, a layer of bubble-wrap plastic underneath the burlap will provide additional insulation.

RAISED BAMBOO BED

The easiest way to change the level in an outside area is with a raised bed. This can divide the space into smaller compartments or provide a base for dense planting to disguise a boundary. A permanent bed can be made from frost-proof bricks, but here a temporary raised bed has been constructed using a wooden box frame with bamboo panels. This will hide a mismatched collection of pots or plastic growing bags, and grouping plants closely together makes watering easier and helps prevent evaporation in hot weather. Inside the box, the pots or growing bags can be raised to the same level on bricks, which will also deter slugs and snails. The softwood frame is coated with a combined wood preservative/stain, chosen to enhance the subtle colors of the rosemary and sage flowers. The corners are constructed with butt joints, so it requires only the most basic carpentry skills.

MATERIALS AND TOOLS

to make a box frame 19½ x 39 in. (50 cm x 1 m)

- 4 each of the following lengths of 2-x 1-in. (5 x 2.5 cm) planed softwood: 39 in (1 m), 12 in. (31 cm), 18 in (45 cm)

- hammer

- corrugated fasteners

- drill

- 2 in. (5 cm) galvanized screws

- screwdriver

- waterproof wood filler

- fine-grade sandpaper

- colored woodstain/preservative

- paintbrush

- 20 bamboo poles, 39 in. (1 m) long

- hacksaw

- galvanized finish nails

Left: Several varieties of mint, rosemary, and sage, planted in individual pots, create the impression of a lush herb garden surrounded by the "sleeve" of a wood and bamboo fence.

1 Construct two sides of the box frame, using two 39-in. (1-m) and two 12-in. (31-cm) lengths of wood. On all four sides, hammer through two corrugated fasteners, catching both pieces of wood to make a perfect right angle. Repeat to make the other side of the frame.

2 Drill two holes at each end of both halves of the frame, then screw on an 18-in. (45-cm) length of wood to form a crosspiece. Repeat with the other three 18-in (45-cm) lengths to make the box. Conceal the screwheads with wood filler, then rub smooth with sandpaper.

3 Paint the frame inside and out with wood preservative/stain and leave to dry. Cut the bamboo into 14 in. (35-cm) lengths, using a hacksaw. (Bamboo tends to splinter, so a fine-toothed blade will give a much cleaner cut.) Pin the bamboo around the inside of the frame, using finish nails.

121

outdoor eating

Eating in the fresh air is quite a different experience from having a meal indoors. Alfresco diners seem to lose track of time, and often a summer lunch lingers on long after the sun has gone down. Enjoying the simple pleasure of home-grown food or the smoky flavors of a barbecue can become an addictive pleasure. Simplicity is the key to such relaxed and memorable occasions.

LEFT A single sprig of garden-grown lavender adds a tiny but very sensitive personal touch to this simply dressed table.

well organized you are, there is always the unpredictable element of the weather. Unlike a gas or electric stove, a wood or charcoal fire will be drastically affected by a strong wind, a damp atmosphere or even the ambient temperature. There are barbecues fueled by gas or electricity, which guarantee successful results every time, but they tend to be bulky and rather ugly.

Outdoor cooking need not be restricted to grilling. The same grill or barbecue can be used to make single-pan dishes such as paella or a fish stew flavored with hot spices or with fresh ginger and lemongrass. If you prefer to cook in the comfort of your own kitchen, you can carry hot dishes outside and place them on basic plate-warmers heated by votives, the kind you often see in Indian restaurants. If you are entertaining in the evening, it is essential to have good overhead lighting to illuminate any steps or paths you may have to negotiate while carrying a hot tureen or tray of glasses.

The outdoor kitchen

It would be inconceivable to design a home without a kitchen, yet many outside spaces are created without even considering the possibility of a place to cook. If a barbecue is being specially built in an outside space, it can be designed following the principles of good kitchen design. Ideally, the cooktop area will be enclosed by two heat-resistant worktops, at approximately hip height, which feel comfortable to work at—barbecuing for a party can be a lengthy affair. If the grill is at waist level, there will be room underneath for storing charcoal or wood chips.

In addition to the cooking area, you need a work surface large enough to take several plates of prepared food ready for cooking. Space should be made for the cooked food, preferably on the other side of the grill. Separating these surfaces avoids the danger of putting cooked food on a plate that has previously held raw meat or fish, which could result in food poisoning.

Above: This is a simple kitchen with the merest basics for outdoor eating and food preparation. It is decorated in the warm and sunny colors of the Mediterranean.

Eating alfresco has to be one of life's greatest pleasures. The best and most memorable outdoor meals are usually the simplest—freshly brewed coffee with warm croissants, a sandwich stuffed with crisp lettuce and a sharp-flavored cheese, or just-caught, well-seasoned fish hot off the barbecue. The fresh air sharpens the appetite, and eating with your hands is a sensual and satisfying experience.

Grilling food over an open fire is the most basic form of outdoor cooking, although it requires some practice to perfect this primeval skill. Some of the finest outdoor food can be cooked merely on a raised metal grill over burning coals, and the secret of success is keeping the recipes simple. If you assemble all the ingredients in advance, this kind of cooking can become an addictive pleasure, but, however

Above: Once the doors to this kitchen are rolled back, the transition between inside and outside is invisible. The open shelving becomes an elegant and practical sideboard.

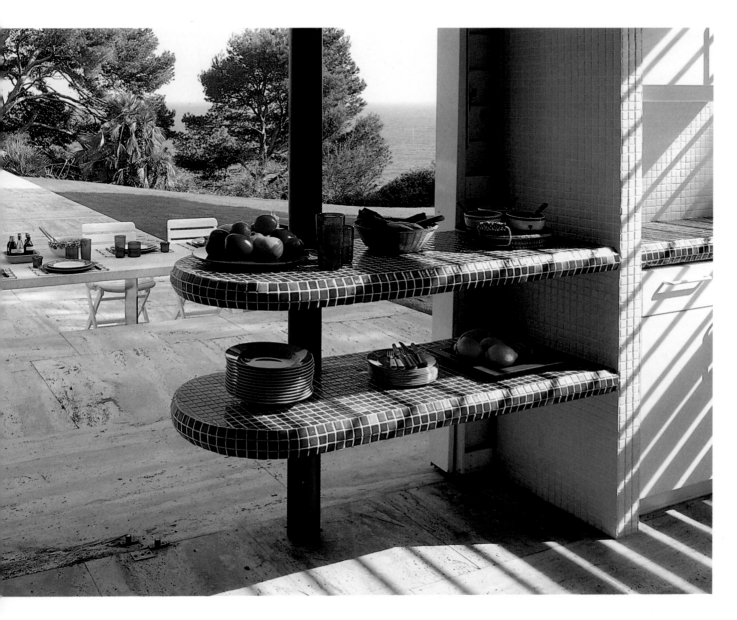

If alfresco barbecues are to be held in the evening, it is essential to provide adequate lighting to cook by and so that your guests can see what they are eating. The grill or barbecue will emit a certain amount of light, but it is impossible to see clearly whether food is cooked without some form of overhead illumination. Provided there is enough space, a sink with running water is always useful. It will allow all the food preparation to be done outdoors, including those messy jobs such as cleaning and gutting fish, washing vegetables and herbs, and cleaning the barbecue after use.

Within easy reach of the outdoor cook should be a basic *batterie de cuisine*. A basting brush will apply oil or glaze; long-handled tongs with a comfortable grip and firm jaws will turn items on the grill; and a flexible metal spatula will lift off the food once it is cooked. Fish-shaped metal baskets allow you to turn grilling fish without any danger of them breaking up, and square or oblong baskets can be used for cooking vegetables. Insulated gauntlets should be used during cooking and for cleaning the grill afterward.

A permanent outdoor area with solid worktops made of heatproof and waterproof materials and with access to running water can be extremely versatile. You can use it for practical gardening tasks such as potting, planting, and sowing seeds and for buffet-style entertaining.

Cooking alfresco

Barbecuing is simple in essence, but in practice it is the most difficult method of cooking perfectly. Once you have cooked regularly on the same barbecue, using the same-quality charcoal, you quickly develop the instinct of knowing exactly when to start putting food on the grill and how long it will take to cook. Modern barbecues are designed to take the guesswork out of heat control, but a bed of glowing charcoal is more difficult to work with. There are no temperature controls on a charcoal barbecue, and that is part of the challenge. It may be great for searing a steak but could completely incinerate the delicate flesh of a fish. Judging when charcoal is fit to cook over can really be determined only by feel and sight.

If you are cooking in daylight, the coals are ready when there are no flames and they have turned gray and started to look powdery. After dark, it is easier to see when there is no flicker of a flame and the coals emit a consistent red glow. When it is impossible to hold your hand over the charcoal for more than a second, the temperature is hot enough to brown the outside of meat but leave the inside rare. Charcoal cooking requires constant attention, and you should never leave open flames unattended.

More control, and therefore more consistent success, can be achieved with a modern barbecue. Cheap, disposable barbecues consist of a self-contained pack containing a heavy foil tray, charcoal, and a wire grid. You have no choice but to wait until the charcoal reaches the optimum temperature before starting to cook. This kind of barbecue will usually burn for about 2 hours and is big enough to cook food for two or three people. Larger, kettle-style barbecues and those built into a stone or brick wall can be fitted with movable grills and adjusted so that they are closer or farther away from the charcoal. The wider area also allows space to spread out the coals and distribute the heat. This can be lowered, to an indeterminate degree, by a squirt of water from a spray bottle. A water spray close at hand is an excellent way of dealing with any actual flames, should they appear.

An important safety precaution is never to position a barbecue close to buildings, wooden fences, plants, or overhanging trees, which could easily get scorched. A strong wind will cause the coals to burn faster and hotter, and gusting winds will create drifting clouds of smoke. A covered barbecue has distinct advantages here, particularly if it has a ventilated lid offering protection from both wind and rain. Barbecues are synonymous with hot summer days and balmy evenings, but there is also something very appealing about cooking outside on a crisp winter's night, serving roasted chestnuts and spicy sausages with mugs of piping hot soup. Potatoes with well-scrubbed skins can be wrapped in foil and cooked in the embers, campfire style. Resist the urge to put too much meat on a barbecue, as the fat will drip onto the coals, and you will be enveloped in a cloud of smoke, unpleasant for you and your guests, not to mention your neighbors.

As an alternative to charcoal, specialist barbecue stores often stock a range of woods such as apple, oak, and mesquite, a wood indigenous to North America and claimed by many to be the finest fuel for barbecuing.

Left: The Zen-inspired oak and steel furniture is offset by warm iroko decking and ocher-colored walls. This creates an intimate dining and cooking area.

The perfect occasion

The secret of successful entertaining is good planning. An outdoor meal is normally leisurely, and the joy of the occasion is its relaxed informality. Aim to prepare all the food in advance, and consider presentation as well as content. In countries where outdoor eating is commonplace, most of the dishes are put on the table at the outset within easy reach of the guests.

All that is needed for a delicious cold meal is a savory flan with seasonal salads, dressed at the last minute, some fine cheeses and wine, and plenty of fresh fruit. If you are cooking on a grill or barbecue, most meat and oily fish, such as sardines, anchovies, mackerel, and herring, need nothing more than seasoning and a light brushing of olive oil. Vegetables such as tomatoes, mushrooms, peppers, onions, and fennel benefit

from a simple marinade of fresh lemon juice, herbs, extra-virgin olive oil, and honey, while ears of corn are best barbecued in their own protective husk. In Indonesia a popular method of grilling fish is to wrap it in banana leaves, which adds to the flavor, although the banana leaves themselves are not edible. Grape vine leaves from the garden or supermarket can be used in the same way and are edible.

Left: A table shaded by a
sailcloth canopy makes a
perfect setting for all-day
dining. Paraffin lamps
add a romantic touch
as evening falls.

Below: This galvanized
metal barbecue is
lightweight and easily
transportable, requiring
a minimal amount of
charcoal; perfect for an
inpromptu meal for two.

Kebabs are very popular at barbecues but need to be prepared in advance, as the process of threading onto skewers is time-consuming. The ingredients for each kebab should have a similar cooking time and be cut to a uniform size, large enough to hold their shape during cooking. Soaking wooden skewers in water overnight will prevent them from burning, and pre-oiling metal skewers will stop the cooked food from sticking.

The difference between a pleasant meal and a really memorable occasion is the finishing touches that make you and your guests feel at ease. If the meal is likely to be a long affair, make sure that the seating is comfortable. Fast-food restaurants reputedly design their seats to become uncomfortable very quickly, and weatherproof outdoor furniture may have the same effect unless the seats and backs are insulated

with a layer of cushioning. Remember also that eating with your fingers is fun and relaxing, provided there are enough napkins and finger bowls within easy reach. Since you can never predict exactly when barbecue food will be ready, ensure that you provide plenty of tasty snacks, salads, and breads, as the aroma from the grill, combined with the open air, will inevitably sharpen the appetite.

ENTERTAINING OUTDOORS

Entertaining alfresco is a wonderful way to share your outside room with family and friends. Choose dishes to suit the season—simple salads, summer fruits, berries, thirst-quenching drinks for hot days, and firm-fleshed fish and seafood cooked over an aromatic barbecue. Prepare as much as possible in advance so you can enjoy and share the experience.

RED, WHITE, AND GREEN SALAD

Cherry tomatoes and quails eggs (available from gourmet food shops and by mail order) combine here with a favorite English salad green, mustard and cress, to make this salad. You can substitute hens' eggs and any kind of lettuce you like.

INGREDIENTS

- ■ quails' eggs and cherry tomatoes
- ■ package of mustard and cress seeds, or any preferred sprouted bean shoots
- ■ large plate with a flat bottom and raised rim
- ■ white paper towel
- ■ plastic wrap
- ■ water spray

1 Cut the paper towel to fit the flat part of the plate. Soak it with fresh, cold water, then sprinkle the seeds evenly over the top. Cover the plate with plastic wrap and place in a warm, dark place.

2 When the seeds have germinated — usually 24–48 hours — remove the plastic, and put the plate near a window with good light. Spray the seeds regularly with water to keep the paper towel moist.

3 Hard-boil the quails' eggs and remove the shells. Place the mustard and cress or lettuce on a serving dish and arrange the quail's eggs and cherry tomatoes in little groups on top.

BARBECUED SHRIMP

Shrimp are the simplest food to barbecue. They take only minutes to cook and are delicious eaten piping hot, dipped in homemade mayonnaise, a tangy salsa, or a spicy peanut sauce. Cooking them on a bed of lemon or lime slices stops the prawns from sticking to the grill, which makes them easier to turn over.

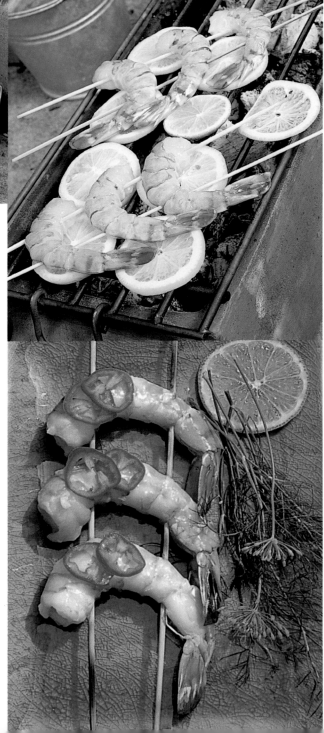

INGREDIENTS

- barbecue and charcoal
- sprigs of rosemary, lavender, or fennel
- fresh raw large shrimp
- wooden skewers, soaked overnight in water
- lemons or limes

1 Light the barbecue well in advance. When all the flames have disappeared, add sprigs of rosemary, lavender, or fennel to create aromatic smoke and deter insects.

2 Meanwhile remove the heads and shells of the shrimp, and the black vein that runs down the back. Wash them in plenty of cold water.

3 Thread each shrimp onto two wooden skewers. Place a layer of lemon or lime slices on the barbecue grill, and lay the shrimp on top. Turn over the skewers after about 2 minutes. The shrimp are cooked when they are pale pink with browned edges. Eat immediately.

ICED BOWLS

These beautiful ice sculptures are very simple to make, and will create an impressive centerpiece for a summer party or special occasion. They melt rapidly but will hold their shape long enough for you to serve home made icecream or sorbet in the center.

If you have flowers in bloom, iced bowls cost absolutely nothing other than your time. Start making them 2 days before you need the bowl.

1 Put a layer of crushed ice in the larger glass bowl. Place the smaller bowl on top, and fill it with marbles or pebbles to weight it down and hold it in place.

2 Fill the gap between the two bowls with a layer of ice, followed by a layer of flowers. Repeat with more alternating layers until you reach the top. Pour in enough chilled water to fill the gaps and up to the top. Freeze for 24 hours.

3 Remove the marbles or pebbles and fill the inside with tepid water, which will release the inner glass bowl. Dip the outer glass bowl in a sink of tepid water until the iced bowl can be gently swiveled away. Return to the freezer.

MATERIALS AND TOOLS

■ crushed ice cubes

■ 2 similar-shaped freezer-proof glass bowls, one smaller than the other

■ marbles or pebbles

■ several handfuls of brightly colored flowerheads

■ pitcher of chilled water

SUMMER FRUIT JELLY

A cake, brioche, or loaf pan makes an excellent jelly mold because metal is the best conductor of heat, which makes it easy to remove the dessert. Freezer-proof, rigid plastic boxes give more contemporary geometric shapes.

Use whole seasonal fruits or large slices. Avoid fresh pineapple and papaya, as these contain an enzyme that breaks down gelatin, and the jelly will refuse to set.

1 Make up the gelatin mixture following the package instructions but substituting white grape juice for water. Use enough gelatin to make a firm jelly.

2 Layer the fruits generously in the mold, packing them firmly around the sides. Pour the cooled jelly liquid over, and refrigerate until completely set.

3 Stand the mold for 20 seconds in a bowl of hot water until the sides of the jelly begin to melt, then invert onto a flat plate. If the jelly does not move, give the mold a firm shake in case there is a vacuum in the top of the mold. Keep the jelly in the refrigerator until ready to serve.

INGREDIENTS

- powdered gelatine

- white grape juice

- selection of fresh fruit, e.g. peaches, nectarines, strawberries, raspberries, blackberries, and redcurrants

- mold

PICKLED CHERRIES

This savory hors d'oeuvre, popular in the south of France, is inspired by a recipe of the British cookery writer, Jane Grigson. It is a wonderful way to use cherries, which make a delicious alternative to olives. They take about a month to mature but can be eaten after 2 weeks.

INGREDIENTS

- 2¾ lb.(1kg) ripe, firm cherries
- sterile preserving jars or plastic-lidded jam jars
- 1 qt.(1 liter) white wine vinegar
- 2½ cups (600g) granulated sugar
- 6 cloves, crushed
- 4 juniper berries, crushed
- zest of 2 lemons
- ¾ in. (2 cm) stick of cinnamon

1 Rinse and dry the cherries, discarding any damaged fruit. Cut the stalks down to about ½ in. (1 cm).

2 Bring the remaining ingredients to the boil in a stainless steel or enameled pan, then simmer for 10 minutes. Leave overnight.

3 Pack the cherries tightly into the jars. Remove the cinnamon stick from the liquid and pour it over the cherries until they are covered; seal.

ICED TEAS

Quench summer thirsts by serving these lightly scented teas, which complement barbecued food and fruity desserts. Lemongrass and mint tea is also delicious served hot with Thai or Chinese food.

INGREDIENTS

For peach tea
- finest Ceylon tea leaves
- ripe peach

For lemongrass and mint tea
- lemongrass stalks
- fresh mint leaves
- extra sprigs of fresh mint

1 To make a peach-flavored tea, infuse the tea leaves with enough boiling water to make a weak tea. Allow to cool. Cut the peach and remove the stone, slice the flesh, add to the tea, and chill.

2 To make lemongrass and mint tea, slice the lemongrass stalks into rounds. Put in a heatproof pitcher with the mint leaves and boiling water. Cool, then chill. Remove the mint leaves and add a few sprigs of mint for decoration.

BURNING LAVENDER STICKS

Lavender is renowned as an insect-repellent, and its essential oil is very soothing for insect bites. When burning, lavender releases a pleasant scent but one unattractive to gnats and mosquitoes. The sticks burn very quickly, so make plenty to last the evening. Stick three or four lavender sticks in an incense burner or improvise by using a bowl filled with sand.

As with lighted candles, you should never leave the burning sticks unattended.

MATERIALS AND TOOLS

- dried lavender

- saltpeter (potassium nitrate), available from herbalists and aromatherapy suppliers

1 Soak the flowerheads and upper stalks of the lavender in a solution of 1 cup warm water and 2 tablespoons saltpeter. Leave for at least an hour.

2 Remove the lavender from the solution. Tie the stalks in a bunch and hang them upside down to dry.

If you are particularly attractive to gnats and mosquitoes, you can protect yourself further by making a sweet-smelling and moisturising oil. Mix 2 drops each of lavender and lemongrass essential oils with ⅓ oz.(10ml) of grapeseed or sweet almond oil. Rub gently onto vulnerable areas such as ankles and wrists.

SOURCES AND MATERIALS

**This listing contains internet-accessible businesses that may be able to supply some of the items used in this book. However, inclusion on this list does not constitute an endorsement of the supplier or their products by the publisher.

Festival International des Jardins
Ferme du Château
41150
Chaumont-sur-Loire
France
tel: 00 33 254 209922
(innovative garden design festival, 185km south of Paris,from mid June–mid October)

Royal Horticultural Society
80 Vincent Square
London
SW1P 2PF
tel: +44 20 7834 4333
(advice, publications and details of RHS garden shows)

WALLS & FLOORS

PAINTED BRICK WALL

Driscoll Masonry Restoration
4502 Jordan Rd.
P.O. Box 219
Skaneateles Falls, NY
13153
tel: (315) 685-5792
website:
www.driscollmasonry.com

Dulux – ICI Paints
Wexham Road
Slough
Berkshire
SL2 5DS
tel: +44 1753 550555
website: www.dulux.com

Farrow & Ball Ltd
33 Uddens Trading Estate
Wimborne
Dorset
BH21 7NL
tel: +44 1202 876141
website: www.farrow-ball.com

National Concrete Masonry Association
2302 Horse Pen Rd.
Herndon, VA
20171-3499
tel: (703) 713-1900
website: www.ncma.org

SLATE WITH TIMBER STEPPING "STONES"

Langley Boxwood Nursery
Rake
Liss
Hampshire
GU33 7JL
tel: +44 1730 894467

Silverland Stone Ltd
Holloway Hill
Lyne
Chertsey
Surrey
KT16 0AE
tel: +44 1932 569277

Vic Hannan Landscape Materials
7086 Highway 273
Anderson, CA
96007
tel: (530) 243-3037
website:
www.vichannan.com

Virginia Slate Co.
Crozet House
100 E. Main St.
Richmond, VA
23219
tel: 1-888-VA-SLATE

FURNITURE & FURNISHINGS

Living.com
1-800-203-7003
website: www.living.com

Good Home Furnishings
website:
www.goodhome.com

Gladly Company
1092 Santiago Dr.
Calexico, CA
92231-4002
tel: (760) 357-1254
website: www.gladly.com

Lake Placid Chair & Garden Company
1477 Turkey Hill Rd.
Northfield, VT
05663
tel: (802) 485-5700
website:
www.lakeplacidchair.com

Smith & Hawken
Locations nationally
tel: 1-800-940-1170
website:
www.smith-hawken.com

Summer Living
website:
www.summerlivingdirect.com

CHAIR COVERS

Crate & Barrel
Locations nationally
tel: 1-800-967-6696
website:
www.crateandbarrel.com

The Furniture Union
65a Hopton Street
London
SE1 9LR
tel: +44 20 7928 5155

Pier 1 Imports
Locations nationally
tel: 1-800-967-6696
website: www.pier1.com

Featherwood Studios
128 Southline Rd.
Middle Grove, NY
12850
tel: (518) 882-1953
website:
www.featherwoodstudios.
home.att.net

Malabar Cotton Company
31–33 South Bank
Business Centre
Ponton Road
London
SW8 5BL
tel: +44 20 7501 4200

TILED TRAY TABLE

Ikea
Locations nationally
tel: 1-800-434-IKEA
website: www.ikea-usa.com

The Reject Tile Shop
178 Wandsworth Bridge
Road
London
SW6 2UQ
tel: +44 20 7731 6098

BURLAP CUSHIONS

Dayton Bag and Burlap
322 Davis Ave
P.O. Box 8
Dayton, OH
45401
tel: 1-800-543-3400
website: www.daybag.com

Dylon International
Worsley Bridge Road
Lower Sydenham
London
SE26 5HD
tel: +44 20 8663 4801
website: www.dylon.co.uk

Farber Bag & Supply Co.
8733 Kapp Dr., P.O. Box 78
Peosta, IA
52068-0078
tel: (319) 583-6304
www.farberbag.com

Colorado Wholesale Dye Corp.
2139 S. Sheridan Blvd.
Denver, CO
80227
tel: 1-800-697-1566
website: www.bestdye.com

FEATURES & FOCAL POINTS

Home Warehouse
tel: 1-877-806-0888
website:
www.homewarehouse.com

Garden Accents
W. Conshohocken,
PA
19428
tel: 1-800-296-5525
website: www.garden-accent.com

Garden Expressions
22627 SR 530 NE
Arlington, WA
98233
tel: 1-888-405-5234
website:
www.gardenexpressions.com

Solaria
4A Pine St.
Avondale Estates, GA
30002
tel: (404) 508-1987
website:
www.solaria-home.com

PAINTED BIRDHOUSE

Jefferson Recycled Woodwork
P.O. Box 696
McCloud, CA
96057
tel: (530) 964-2740
website:
www.ecowood.com

LASSCo
St Michael's Church
Mark Street
London
EC2A 4ER
tel: +44 20 7739 0448
website:
www.lassco.co.uk

The Old Fashioned Milk Paint Company
436 Main St.
Groton, MA
01450
website:
www.milkpaint.com

Vintage Barns, Woods & Restorations
333 Mossy
Brook Road.
High Falls, NY
12440
tel: (914) 340-9870
website:
www.vintagewoods.com

Trestlewood
933 S. Frontage Rd.
Blackfoot, ID
tel: (208) 785-1152
www.trestlewood.com

RUSTIC MIRROR

See reference for reclaimed lumber in Painted Birdhouse

Liberon Waxes Ltd
Learoyd Road
Mountfield Industrial Estate
New Romney
Kent
TN28 8XU
tel: +44 1797 367555

Mann Woodcare
P.O. Box 343
E. Winthrop, ME
04343
tel: (207) 395-2739
website:
www.mannwoodcare.com

LIGHTING

RECYCLED GLASS LANTERN

Ark Lighting
11646 W. Pico Blvd.
Los Angeles, CA
90064
tel: 1-888-275-5444
website:
www.arklighting.com

Container Recycling Alliance
8725 West Higgins Rd.
Suite 485
Chicago, IL
60631
fax: (773) 714-9764
website: www.craglass.com

Contractors Tools.com
website:
www.contractorstools.com

Price's Patent Candle Company Ltd
110 York Road
London
SW11 3RU
tel: +44 20 7228 3345

SCENTED CHANDELIER

Avant Garden
The Studio
3 Dartmouth Place
London
W4 2RH
tel: 020 8994 0793

Lighting Universe
tel: 1-888-404-2744
website:
www.lightinguniverse.com

Noma Lites Ltd
Southey House
Vickers Drive
North Brooklands
Industrial Park
Weybridge
Surrey
KT13 0YU
tel: +44 1932 411330

Spectrum Home Lighting
tel: (732) 460-0664

Wilkinson plc
5 Catford Hill
London
SE6 4NU
tel: +44 20 8314 1080

WATER

CONTAINER POND

Chairworks
Units 77
Chelsea Bridge
Business Centre
Queenstown Road
London
SW8 4NE
tel: +44 20 7498 7611

Ductaire Fabrications
Unit G
23 Grafton Road
West Croydon
Surrey
CR0 3RP
tel: +44 20 8688 5188

Oase UK
2 North Way
Walworth Industrial
Estate
Andover
Hampshire
SP10 3SF
tel: +44 1264 333225

Planned Environmental Services
Wealden Barn,
Bethersden Road
Smarden
Kent
TN27 8QF
tel: +44 1233 770795

BUBBLE FOUNTAINS

Beth Chatto Gardens
White Barn House
Clacton Road
Elmstead
Essex
C07 7DB
tel: +44 1206 822007

Lake Fountains & Aeration
Sanford, FL
tel: 1-800-353-5253
website:
www.lakefountains.com

Long Island Fountain Co.
10-2 Drew Court
Ronkonkoma, NY
11779
tel: (613) 467-5115
website: www.lifountain.com

Maryland Aquatic Nurseries
3427 N. Furnace Rd.
Jarretsville, MD
21084
tel: (410) 557-7615
website:
www.marylandaquatic.com

Ponds, Pools & Fountains
5508 Elmwod Ave, Suite 411
Indianapolis, IN
46203
tel: 1-800-651-0002
website: www.ppfc.com

Split Rock Ponds
Monmouth County, NJ
tel: 1-800-352-7826
website:
www.walnet.com/splitrock/

Van Ness Water Garden
2460 N. Euclid Ave.
Upland, CA
91784-1199
tel: 1-800-205-2425
website: www.vnwg.com

Water Gardens Galore
4236 W. Lovers Lane
Dallas, TX
75209-2820
tel: (214) 956-7382
website:www.wggalore.com

Windmill Aggregates
Windmill Works
Aythorpe Roding,
Dunmow
Essex
CM6 1PQ
tel: 01279 876987

DECORATING WITH PLANTS

DECORATED POTS

Great Bay Trellises
Greenland, NH
tel: (603) 431-6798
website:
www.wroughtirontrellis.com

Avant Garden
(see reference in Scented
Chandelier section)

Anamese Garden Pots
18080 La Motte Rd.
Welsh, LA
70591
tel: (337) 734-3656
website: www.anamese.com

Cempak Ltd
Forge Lane
Thornhill Lees
Dewsbury
West Yorkshire
WF12 9BU
tel: +44 1924 452644

Potmolen Paint
27 Woodcock
Industrial Estate
Warminster
Wiltshire
BA12 9DX
tel: +44 1985 213960

TWO-TIER CONTAINER

Fibrex Nurseries
Honeybourne Road
Pebworth
Warwickshire
CV37 8XP
tel: +44 1789 720788

**Gardener's Supply
Company**
128 Intervale Rd.
Burlington, VT
05401
tel: 1-800-863-1700
website:
www.gardeners.com

The Home Depot
Locations nationally
website:
www.homedepot.com

Garden Escape
website: www.garden.com

Logee's Greenhouse
141 North St.
Danielson, CT
06239-1939
tel: 1-888-330-8038
website:
www.logees.com

Willow Pond Nursery
P.O. Box 192
Hewlett, NY
tel: (516) 374-2522
website:
www.willowpondnursery.com

RAISED BAMBOO BED

**Cane & Basket Supply
Company**
1283 Cochran Ave.
Los Angeles, CA
90019
tel: (323) 939-9644

Burton's Bamboo Garden
website:
www.burtonsbamboogarden.
com

The Cane Store
207 Blackstock Road
London
N5 2LL
tel: +44 20 7354 4210

Herb Specialists
Goodwood,
Ontario L0C 1A0
tel: (905) 640-6677
website:
www.richters.com

Johnny's Selected Seeds
Foss Hill Road
Albion, ME
04190
tel: (207) 437-4395
website:
www.johnnyseeds.com

World Seed
300 Morning Drive
Bakersfield, CA
93306
website:
www.worldseed.com

**ENTERTAINING
OUTDOORS**

Cook's Garden
P.O. Box 5010
Hodges, SC
29653-5010
tel: 1-800-457-9703
website:
www.cooksgarden.com

INDEX

ACKNOWLEDGMENTS

I would like to thank Linda Burgess for her inspirational pictures; Sue Storey for her sensitive design; and Emma Clegg and Liz Boyd at Conran Octopus for their support and enthusiasm. Many of the design projects in this book were recreated with the skills and expertise of Helen and Andrew Fickling, Steven Gott, Valerie Barrett, Geoffrey Love, and Cally Law, as well as Frank Parr at Dylon, Rosemary Titterington at Iden Croft Herbs, Mike Wilderink and John Anderson at the Outdoor Deck Company, and Simon Harman and Hayley John at Lilies Water Gardens—my special thanks to you all.

The publisher would like to thank the following photographers and agencies for their kind permission to reproduce the photographs in this book.

2–3 Francesca Giovanelli; 4–5 Mirjam Bleeker/Taverne Agency and Frank Visser; 8 J C Mayer–G Le Scanff/Festival des Jardins de Chaumont-Sur-Loire, France (Designers: E. Jalbert & A. Tardivon); 10–11 Anneke de Leeuw/Taverne Agency; 11 Marijke Heuff(Jardin De'Coursel, France); 12 Richard Bryant (Architect: Spencer Fung)/Arcaid; 12–13 Ross Honeysett; 14–15 Mirjam Bleeker/Taverne Agency and Frank Visser; 15 Gil Hanly (Designers: Ted Smyth and Ron Sang); 16 Winfried Heinz; 17 above Helen Fickling; 17 below Helen Fickling; 18 Garry Sarre (Designers: Stephan and Simon Rodrigues Stylist: Anne-Louise Willoughby)/Belle/Arcaid; 19 above Jerry Harpur (Designer: Fred Mengoni, NYC/Harpur Garden Library); 19 below Andrew Lawson (Designer: Dan Pearson); 20 Henk Dijkman; 21 Santi Caleca; 22–23 Melanie Eclare (Designers: Tindale Batstone); 24 Jerry Harpur (Designers: Jean-Marc Bourry, Marc Soucat, Chaumont Festival 1999)/Harpur Garden Library; 25 above Howard Sooley (Artist: Derek Jarman); 25 below J C Mayer–G Le Scanff/Festival des Jardins Chaumont-sur-Loire (Designer: Thomas Boog and Patrick Bailly); 26 Peter Anderson; 28 Verne Fotografie (A.Vereecke); 30 Mark Burgin/*Vogue Living*; 31 Helen Fickling (Designer: DeWet Loww, South Africa); 32 Beatrice Pichon-Clarisse (Designer: H. Peuvergne); 33 above Helen Fickling; 33 below Lanny Provo; 34 J C Mayer–G Le Scanff/Jardin des Paradis, Cordes su Ciel, France (Designers: E. Ossart & A. Maurieres); 34–35 Richard Bryant/Arcaid; 36 left Sunniva Harte (Designer: Goodman Portland); 36 right Andrew Lawson (Designer: Kate Collity); 37 Nicola Browne (Designer: Avant Gardener with Garden Design); 38 Melanie Eclare (Designers: Tindale Batstone); 38–39 Gil Hanly (Designer: Robin Curnaham); 39 Helen Fickling(Artist:Prinsloo) /The Interior Archive; 44 Marianne Majerus (Designer: Sarah Chrisp); 46 Undine Prohl (Architect: Ricardo Legorreta); 46–47 Marie Pierre Morel (Stylist: Christine Puech)/Marie Claire Maison; 48 Helen Fickling/The Interior Archive; 49 above Juliette Wade; 49 below Hannah Lewis/Living Etc/IPC Syndication; 50-51 Geoff Lung/Belle Magazine; 52 left J C Mayer - G Le Scanff/Festival des Jardins de Chaumont sur Loire, France(Designer: Eric Ossart); 52 right Helen Fickling; 53 Willem Rethmeier/*Vogue Living*; 60 Andrew Wood (Designer: Philip Hooper)/The Interior Archive; 62 Marijke Heuff (Designer: Mein Ruys); 63 Juliette Wade (Priory D'orsan, France); 64–65 Marijke Heuff (Jardin La Casella, France); 65 Andrew Lawson (Old Rectory, Sudborough, Northants); 66 Michele Lamontagne (Designer: Martha Schwartz); 67 Jerry Harpur (Designer: Nancy Heckler)/Harpur Garden Library; 68 above J C Mayer–G Le Scanff/Festival des Jardins de Chaumont-sur-Loire, France (Designers: C.Cheick-Gonzalez & I Ropelato); 68 below Georgia Glynn-Smith/The Garden Picture Library; 69 Helen Fickling (Artist: Prinsloo)/The Interior Archive; 76 Georgie Cole/*Vogue Entertaining & Travel*; 78 left Andrew Lawson (Designer: Ivan Hicks); 78 right Andrew Lawson; 79 Andrew Lawson; 80 above Guy Bouchet (Stylist: Bayle/Puech)/*Marie Claire Maison*; 80 below J C Mayer–G Le Scanff/Jardin des Paradis, Cordes sur Ciel, France (Designers: E. Ossart & A. Maurieres); 80–81 J C Mayer–G Le Scanff/Jardins des Fournials, France (Designers: E. Ossart & A. Maurierers); 82 Earl Carter (Architect: Andrew Nolan)/Belle/Arcaid; 83 above Nicola Browne (Designer: Martha Schwartz); 83 below Reiner Blunck (Architect: Martin Wagner); 92–93 Reiner Blunck (Architect: Glenn Murcutt); 93 above Alexandre Bailhache (Stylist: Anne-Marie Comte)/*Marie Claire Maison*; 93 below Winfried Heinz; 94 Andrew Lawson; 94–95 Jerry Harpur (Designer: Ken Ruzicka, NYC)/Harpur Garden Library; 96 Mise au Point/Chaumont 97; 96–97 Andrea Jones (Channel 4 Garden Doctors Series 99); 97 Melanie Eclare (Designers: Tindale Batstone); 104 Andrea Jones (Yves Saint Laurent Garden, Chelsea); 106 Marijke Heuff; 107 left Jerry Harpur (Designer: Jeff Mendoza)/Harpur Garden Library; 107 right J C Mayer–G Le Scanff/Festival des Jardins de Chaumont-sur-Loire (Designer: Eric Ossart); 108 Andrew Lawson; 108–109 J C Mayer–G Le Scanff/Festival des Jardins de Chaumont-sur-Loire (Designers: F di Carlo & M Sgandurra); 110 Marianne Majerus (Designer: Ruth Collier); 110–111 Henk Dijkman; 112 Marcus Harpur (Designer: Beth Chatto, Essex)/Harpur Garden Library; 113 above Nicola Browne (Designers: Avant Gardener with Garden Design); 113 below Jerry Harpur (Designer: Dan Pearson, London)/Harpur Garden Library (Designer: Dan Pearson); 122 James Merrell/*Homes & Gardens*/IPC Syndication; 124 Marie Pierre Morel/*Marie Claire Maison*; 124-125 Dexter Hodges (Stylist: Ino Coll)/*La Casa de Marie Claire*; 126–127 Martin Morrel/*Elle Decoration*; 128–129 Hotze Eisma/*Living*/VNU Syndication; 129 Simon Brown/The Interior Archive

Every effort has been made to trace the copyright holders and we apologise in advance for any unintentional omission and would be pleased to insert the appropriate acknowledgment in any subsequent edition.